THE HISTORY CHANNEL.

# the states

INTRIGUING TALES ABOUT THE BUILDING BLOCKS OF A NATION

**PUBLISHED, EDITED & DESIGNED BY**
Journey Group, Inc.
418 Fourth Street, NE
Charlottesville VA 22902-4722
434 961-2500
www.journeygroup.com

**THIS BOOK IS PUBLISHED AND LICENSED IN COOPERATION WITH**
A&E Television Networks &
THE HISTORY CHANNEL®
235 East 45th Street
New York NY 10017-3305
and
UNITED STATES POSTAL SERVICE
475 L'Enfant Plaza, SW
Washington DC 20260-2200

Library of Congress Number: 2007928469
ISBN: 978-0-9796569-0-3

**TO ORDER EXTRA COPIES OF THIS LIMITED EDITION COLLECTION:**

| | |
|---|---|
| Online: | www.usps.com/shop or |
| | www.ShopHistoryChannel.com |
| Phone: | 1 800 STAMP-24 (1 800 782-6724) |
| Mail: | United States Postal Service |
| | Stamp Fulfillment Services |
| | PO Box 7247 |
| | Philadelphia PA 19101-7097 |

The information in this book is true and complete to the best of our
knowledge and is expressed without guarantee on the part of the publisher.

THE HISTORY CHANNEL.

the states

INTRIGUING TALES ABOUT THE BUILDING BLOCKS OF A NATION

| CONTENTS | PAGE | DVD |
|---|---|---|

102 WASHINGTON

60 MONTANA

82 OREGON

32 IDAHO

108 WYOMING

64 NEVADA

96 UTAH

20 COLORADO

18 CALIFORNIA

14 ARIZONA

70 NEW MEXICO

12 ALASKA

30 HAWAII

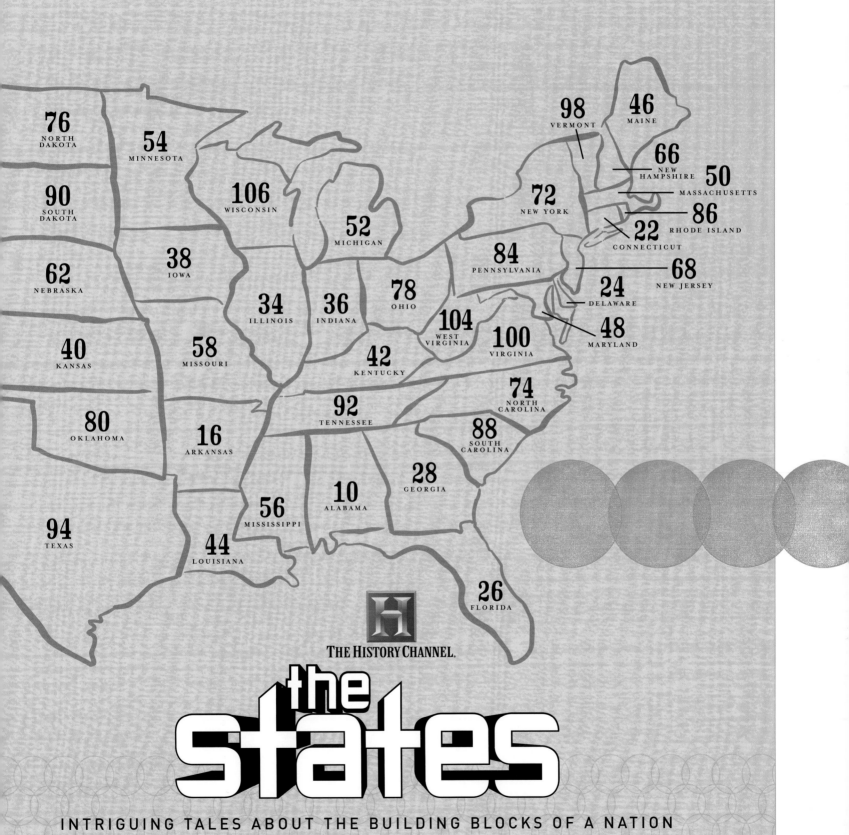

**76** NORTH DAKOTA

**54** MINNESOTA

**90** SOUTH DAKOTA

**62** NEBRASKA

**40** KANSAS

**80** OKLAHOMA

**94** TEXAS

**106** WISCONSIN

**38** IOWA

**34** ILLINOIS

**58** MISSOURI

**16** ARKANSAS

**44** LOUISIANA

**56** MISSISSIPPI

**52** MICHIGAN

**36** INDIANA

**78** OHIO

**42** KENTUCKY

**92** TENNESSEE

**10** ALABAMA

**28** GEORGIA

**26** FLORIDA

**88** SOUTH CAROLINA

**74** NORTH CAROLINA

**104** WEST VIRGINIA

**100** VIRGINIA

**84** PENNSYLVANIA

**72** NEW YORK

**98** VERMONT

**46** MAINE

**66** NEW HAMPSHIRE

**50** MASSACHUSETTS

**86** RHODE ISLAND

**22** CONNECTICUT

**68** NEW JERSEY

**24** DELAWARE

**48** MARYLAND

THE HISTORY CHANNEL.

# the states

INTRIGUING TALES ABOUT THE BUILDING BLOCKS OF A NATION

Welcome to this collection of varied and often surprising stories about our nation. Explore the sweeping themes that shaped our history — the colonies' struggle for independence, the Midwest's battle to conquer the land or the pioneering exploits that opened up the West. These are the crucial building blocks for the nation.

Uncover the cultural nuances that flavor each individual state and its inhabitants. For example, which state was once a worldwide wine-making center . . . until Prohibition? Which state has a highway named for extraterrestrials? And which state has the only capital not accessible by road?

Discover these fascinating stories, and more, in *The States: Intriguing Tales About the Building Blocks of a Nation* and its accompanying DVD set of THE HISTORY CHANNEL® series, "The States," included in the back of this book. This first-ever collaboration between THE HISTORY CHANNEL and the U.S. POSTAL SERVICE also includes a pane of 50 *Greetings From America* stamps, first issued in 2002 and now featured in this collection. Each stamp design is reminiscent of the retro postcards popular with tourists in the 1930s and '40s.

Open the book or watch the series, and embark on a tour of our remarkable national heritage.

2002

## //////// THE YELLOWHAMMER STATE

This state has produced numerous sports greats and music legends and is also known for its historic role in the Civil Rights Movement. Alabama's past sports heroes include Jesse Owens, Joe Louis, Hank Aaron and Willie Mays. Helen Keller was born here as well and is memorialized on the 2003 state quarter. Few outsiders know that Alabama's nickname stems from the Civil War, when battle-weary Confederates mocked fresh recruits from Huntsville for the bright, yellow cloth of their new uniforms. The yellowhammer is also the state bird.

A music boom came to the obscure town of Muscle Shoals in the late 1950s with the opening of FAME Recording Studio®. A decade later, FAME's rhythm section broke away to become Muscle Shoals Sound Studio℠. Artists who recorded there include legends Aretha Franklin, Wilson Pickett, Bob Seger, Paul Simon and the Rolling Stones. *Greetings from Alabama* — deep in the heart of Dixie.

Yellowhammer

# the bus boycott

ALABAMA IS KNOWN AS a fiercely independent state. Although not the first to leave the Union (it ranked fourth), it's considered the birthplace of the Confederacy. In 1923, that fighting spirit was captured in the state's motto, *Audemus Jura Nostra Defendere* ("We Dare Defend Our Rights"). In an ironic twist, a 42-year-old seamstress became perhaps the most famous Alabaman to live up to that motto.

Jim Crow laws were firmly entrenched across the state in 1955, when Rosa Parks refused to give up her seat to a white passenger on a Montgomery bus. Her action, and subsequent arrest, led to the famous Montgomery Bus Boycott, which lasted more than a year. Leading the boycott was a young Martin Luther King Jr., and the Civil Rights Movement gained new momentum.

## We will not secede

ALABAMA'S CURRENT CAPITAL, Montgomery, served as the first capital of the Confederacy during the Civil War. But not all Alabamans believed that the South's cause was just. People in the Appalachian foothills rarely owned slaves. So the folks in Winston County decided that if Alabama had a right to secede from the Union, they had a right to secede from Alabama. Winston County's secession movement fell apart, however, after its leader was arrested. To this day, the area is known colloquially as the "Free State of Winston."

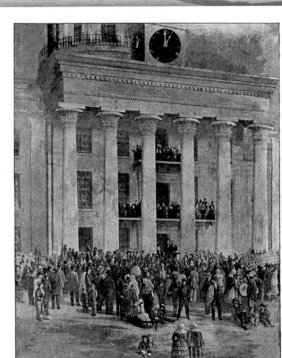

2002

## THE LAST FRONTIER

**Welcome to the land of extremes: the state with the highest mountain, least amount of daylight, largest spread of land and lowest population density. In fact, if Manhattan had as few people per square mile as Alaska, you'd only find about 25 people walking its streets. And speaking of streets, did you know that you can't reach Juneau, the state capital, by road at all?**

**Few people also know that in early June 1942, Japanese forces occupied two islands at the far end of the Aleutian chain, marking the first (and only) invasion of U.S. soil since the War of 1812. After a year of Japanese occupation, U.S. forces launched a bloody offensive that resulted in the deaths of 549 Americans and approximately 2,300 Japanese in what became known as "The Forgotten Campaign." *Greetings from Alaska* — the state purchased from Imperial Russia for about 2 cents an acre. Such a deal.**

Soldiers on the Aleutian Islands

# The Great Alaskan Pipeline

GETTING THINGS FROM *here* to *there* when many would say "impossible" actually defines the frontier spirit of Alaska. So when huge quantities of oil were discovered under Prudhoe Bay in 1968, engineers went to work to make another impossible feat come true. The challenge: transport fuel across 800 miles of mountains, ice and the mighty Yukon River to the nearest port, while protecting the Arctic wilderness.

A pipeline was the only solution: a 48-inch-wide, 800-mile-long pipeline with special engineering considerations so that the hot oil wouldn't melt the permanently frozen ground. Construction on the TransAlaska Pipeline System began in March 1975. Twenty-six months and $8 billion later, the project was completed. Since then, an average of 1.3 million barrels a day have been pumped across some of the most remote and spectacular scenery in the world.

# DOG Sledding

DURING THE GOLD-RUSH years at the turn of the 19th century, dog sleds were the vehicle of choice for transporting people, mail and critical supplies during months when roads were inaccessible. They carried even more precious cargo too: In 1925, when a diphtheria epidemic threatened Nome, Alaska, dog-sled teams delivered lifesaving serum, in relay-fashion, over hundreds of miles from the railhead to the snowbound city.

But with the advent of modern aviation, dog sledding returned to more localized, less-critical uses. In 1973, to both preserve and honor the state's unique tradition, Alaskans initiated the Iditarod Trail Sled Dog Race®: 12 to 16 dogs pulling each sled over more than 1,150 miles. The Iditarod commemorates the crucial role that sled dogs played in the settlement of Alaska.

# THE GRAND CANYON STATE

Where in America might you find one state with both the hottest and coldest temperatures — on the same day? Welcome to Arizona, averaging an annual snowfall of almost 250 inches and proclaimed "sunniest state" by the National Weather Service (with an all-time high in 1994 of 128 degrees). This state also boasts 330 golf courses, which help attract millions of visitors each year.

But perhaps the world knows Arizona best for its state treasure: the Grand Canyon. This landmark always makes the short list of the world's "natural wonders." Visitors must agree. Each year, almost 5 million of them marvel at what they can see of its depth (averaging 4,000 feet), width (15 miles at its widest point) and length (277 miles). The site received National Park status in 1919. *Greetings from Arizona* — the state with more high-powered telescopes than anywhere else in the nation.

Grand Canyon

**37 USA** *Greetings from* ARIZONA

2002

14

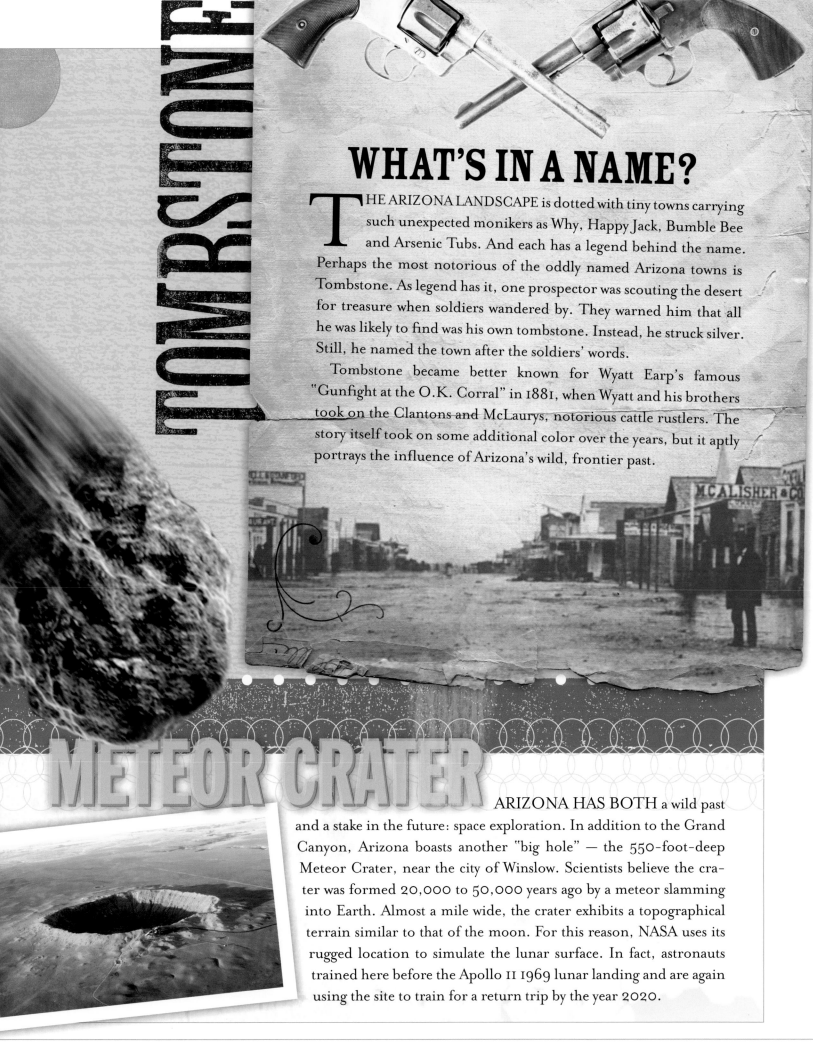

# TOMBSTONE

## WHAT'S IN A NAME?

THE ARIZONA LANDSCAPE is dotted with tiny towns carrying such unexpected monikers as Why, Happy Jack, Bumble Bee and Arsenic Tubs. And each has a legend behind the name. Perhaps the most notorious of the oddly named Arizona towns is Tombstone. As legend has it, one prospector was scouting the desert for treasure when soldiers wandered by. They warned him that all he was likely to find was his own tombstone. Instead, he struck silver. Still, he named the town after the soldiers' words.

Tombstone became better known for Wyatt Earp's famous "Gunfight at the O.K. Corral" in 1881, when Wyatt and his brothers took on the Clantons and McLaurys, notorious cattle rustlers. The story itself took on some additional color over the years, but it aptly portrays the influence of Arizona's wild, frontier past.

## METEOR CRATER

ARIZONA HAS BOTH a wild past and a stake in the future: space exploration. In addition to the Grand Canyon, Arizona boasts another "big hole" — the 550-foot-deep Meteor Crater, near the city of Winslow. Scientists believe the crater was formed 20,000 to 50,000 years ago by a meteor slamming into Earth. Almost a mile wide, the crater exhibits a topographical terrain similar to that of the moon. For this reason, NASA uses its rugged location to simulate the lunar surface. In fact, astronauts trained here before the Apollo 11 1969 lunar landing and are again using the site to train for a return trip by the year 2020.

Greetings from ARKANSAS

USA 37

2002

David Owen Dodd

//////// THE NATURAL STATE With more than 600,000 acres of lakes, this state attracts sportsmen from around the world. It possesses other outstanding natural resources as well. In Crater of Diamonds State Park, for example, if you mine a gem from the ground, you can keep it. And when it comes to worldwide influence, Arkansas has it: birthplace of both America's 42nd president, Bill Clinton, and the world's largest retailer, Wal-Mart®.

The outside world began flocking to Hot Springs soon after the region became U.S. territory in 1803, as part of the Louisiana Purchase. The attraction: mineral-rich thermal baths believed to have therapeutic value. Major-league baseball teams scheduled spring training there. And mobsters from Chicago and New York, such as Al Capone and Bugs Moran, deemed it "neutral territory" for their vacations. *Greetings from Arkansas* — where nearly half the land is still in its natural state.

# The Boy Martyr of the South

IN ADDITION TO scenic beauty, Arkansas lays claim to more than 750 military engagements during the Civil War — thanks to its strategic location on the Mississippi River. Of all people involved in the conflict, at least one stands out: 17-year-old David Owen Dodd. In late December 1863, Dodd was returning from a business errand for his father when he was stopped at a Union checkpoint. In his possession was a memorandum book with messages in Morse code, detailing the locations and strengths of Union defensive positions in Little Rock.

Dodd was arrested and charged with spying for the Confederacy, then tried and found guilty. After he refused to divulge other names, Dodd was hanged on January 8, 1864, before a crowd of nearly 6,000. Volunteers still tend his grave at the Mt. Holly Cemetery in Little Rock.

# THE LITTLE ROCK NINE

Central High School

Little Rock Nine Memorial

In early 1957, Little Rock's school board voted to integrate its school system, but not everyone was ready to accept desegregation. The day before classes started at Central High School, Gov. Orval Faubus called out the Arkansas National Guard, with orders to prevent violence. As a result, the nine African-American students were prevented from entering. Their second attempt was also thwarted.

President Eisenhower eventually sent in the 101st Airborne Rangers, and the students successfully entered the school on September 23, 1957. Eight of the nine students completed the year, despite physical and verbal abuse.

A civil-rights museum now stands next door to Central High School. In 1999, each of the Little Rock Nine was awarded the nation's highest civilian honor: the Congressional Gold Medal. In 2005, a monument to the students was unveiled on the State Capitol grounds.

Greetings from CALIFORNIA
USA 37
2002

//////////// **THE GOLDEN STATE** California is the birthplace of trends and ground zero for cool. The most populous state, at more than 36 million, it's still growing fast. California is also incredibly diverse: One of every four residents was born in another country.

Many of the state's cultural innovations were driven by a love affair with the car. An affluent state with little mass-transit infrastructure, California is tied together by ribbons of highway. On some days, a Californian can snow ski in the morning and surf in the afternoon (or, more likely, get stuck in traffic in between). Although they drive about the same number of miles annually as the average American, Californians spend more time in their cars — thanks largely to recent population growth that has outpaced high-way construction. *Greetings from California* — the nation's leading producer of fruits and vegetables, not to mention wine and movie stars.

OCT *California* CAR CULTURE

# GOLD RUSH

THE DISCOVERY OF GOLD at Sutter's Mill in January 1848 swelled the state's population and the world's imagination. The territory's non-Native American population increased by more than 200,000 in just four years, bringing fortune hunters by ship and wagon train from as far away as Australia, China and the eastern United States. Though surface-based sources of gold were largely exhausted by 1864, the California Gold Rush transformed expectations about the state — still viewed today as a land of instant success.

# San Francisco Earthquake

CALIFORNIA'S VISION of paradise was rocked to the core on April 18, 1906, when an earthquake centered in San Francisco killed hundreds of people and destroyed thousands of buildings. The strongest tremors lasted only about a minute — but resulting fires burned for days, and the impact was measured as far away as Germany.

At an estimated magnitude of 8.25 by today's standards, that earthquake ranks among the most powerful ever to strike the state.

Since then, the threat of earthquakes has been an ever-present reality. The San Andreas Fault runs down the length of the state like a scar. Every time an earthquake strikes, a few thousand people move away. But they are soon replaced by the tremors of other moving vans bringing new residents to the Golden State.

**With more than 50 of its peaks** topping the 14,000-foot mark, Colorado is often compared to Switzerland. Its most famous pinnacle is Pike's Peak — immortalized by an English teacher in the 1890s, who found in it the inspiration to write "America, the Beautiful." Denver's mountains and snow made it an obvious selection for the 1976 Winter Olympic Games; not as obvious was that Colorado voters would turn down the honor, citing environmental concerns. Colorado's nickname is derived from the year it achieved statehood: 1876, America's centennial.

Colorado is also famous for the U.S. Air Force Academy, and less famous for housing the only super maximum-security federal prison and some of its high-profile criminals: Unabomber Ted Kaczynski; 1995 Oklahoma City bombing conspirator Terry Nichols; and 9/11 conspirator Zacarias Moussaoui.

*Greetings from Colorado* — believed to be the birthplace of America's first organized rodeo.

Greetings from COLORADO

2002

# NORAD

IN THE 1950S, WITH THE COLD WAR heating up and the nuclear-arms race in full swing, the United States and Canada chose Colorado as the location for a unique joint operation in the event of Soviet attack: North American Aerospace Defense Command, or NORAD. In 1966, NORAD opened its command-and-control center in a massive, fortified bunker situated 2,400 feet below the ground near Cheyenne Mountain, just outside Colorado Springs. Since then, NORAD's emphasis has shifted as world tensions have shifted: from Cold War concerns to drug-trafficking alerts, to the monitoring of domestic airspace in case of terrorist attacks.

# THE DENVER MINT

WHO WOULD HAVE IMAGINED that the inauspicious name of "Clark, Gruber & Company" would serve as the foundation for one of the world's most respected institutions? In 1859, Clark, Gruber & Company opened as a private bank in Denver, shortly before the gold and silver boom that lured thousands of fortune seekers. The bank began buying gold dust from miners and turning it into $2.50, $5, $10 and $20 gold pieces. Then, in 1863, the U.S. Treasury acquired the bank and reopened it as a government operation. Today, the Denver Mint issues an average of 50 million coins each day, which it claims as the world's record. So the next time you get a quarter, look for a small D on the front — the mark of the Denver Mint.

Greetings from *Connecticut*

USA 37

2002

////////// **THE CONSTITUTION STATE** England's Charles II granted this colony an official charter in 1662, but a quarter-century later, King James II changed his mind and ordered Connecticut to be swallowed up into a single New England province. When the appointed governor showed up to reclaim the royal charter, it was hidden in a giant oak tree. The document was never returned to the king; and the tree, called the "Charter Oak," became an enduring symbol of Connecticut's spirit of independence.

Connecticut claims its nickname from "The Fundamental Orders," adopted by three towns in 1639 and believed to be the first written constitution — a claim disputed by some historians (probably out-of-staters).

*Greetings from Connecticut* — where a sandwich shop redefined dining by inventing the hamburger, and Yale students redefined university life by inventing the Frisbee®.

22

# *Insurance City*

CONNECTICUT'S ENDURING MARITIME TRADITIONS led to the state's largest industry: insurance. As more ships set sail for ports around the world, merchants became concerned about the risks of pirates, storms and accidents. Groups of merchants decided to share the risk, and the state's insurance industry was born in Hartford.

Despite its roots in shipbuilding, Connecticut's insurance industry rose to the forefront nationally after a land-based event in another state. In December 1835, a fire spread through New York City's financial district and bankrupted all but three of the city's fire-insurance companies. Hartford's insurance companies aided in New York's recovery, which helped establish Hartford as the insurance capital of the world. Over the years, Hartford insurers have protected such assets as the Golden Gate Bridge, the Hoover Dam and Babe Ruth's baseball earnings.

# SAILS TO SUBS

CONNECTICUT'S SOUTHERN border, the Long Island Sound, has deep water and easy access to the Atlantic. Thus, the sea has been the lifeblood of much of Connecticut's economy. Protected ports and easy access to timber made the state an early hub for shipbuilding, dating back to the majestic sailing ships of earlier centuries. But the state still leads in one of the most high-tech corridors of shipbuilding: submarines.

Connecticut's David Bushnell created the first submarine used in wartime. The one-manned "Turtle" was used in an unsuccessful attempt to sink a British warship in 1776. In the 1940s, the 74 subs launched from Electric Boat's Groton plant accounted for 39 percent of all Japanese subs sunk during World War II. The Cold War brought further innovation with the world's first nuclear-powered submarines, which can function underwater for months at a time.

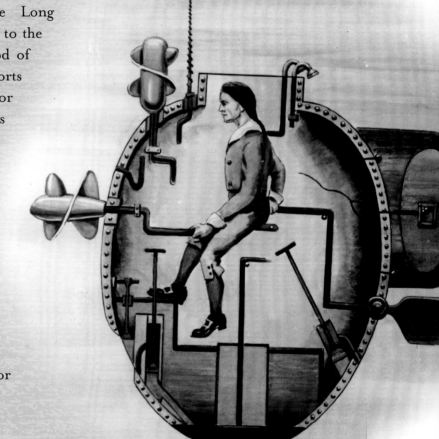

The one-manned "Turtle"

**DELAWARE**

USA **37**

2002

## ////////// THE FIRST STATE

When the United States got started as a nation, Delaware arrived first. Because Delaware was the first to adopt the U.S. Constitution, it lays claim to being the very first state. As a result, with every presidential inauguration, Delaware marches first in the parade. Delaware is small, but it packs corporate power. Over half of the Fortune 500 companies are incorporated here, among more than 500,000 corporate entities statewide. Within a decade, there could be one business entity for every person in the state. *Greetings from Delaware* — where there is no sales tax and no personal-property tax.

# DUPONT® AND GUNPOWDER

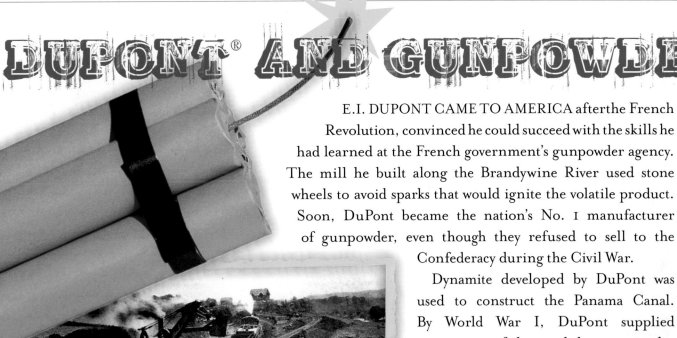

E.I. DUPONT CAME TO AMERICA after the French Revolution, convinced he could succeed with the skills he had learned at the French government's gunpowder agency. The mill he built along the Brandywine River used stone wheels to avoid sparks that would ignite the volatile product. Soon, DuPont became the nation's No. 1 manufacturer of gunpowder, even though they refused to sell to the Confederacy during the Civil War.

Dynamite developed by DuPont was used to construct the Panama Canal. By World War I, DuPont supplied 40 percent of the smokeless gunpowder used by the Allies. Throughout the 20th century, DuPont continued to expand, becoming one of the largest chemical companies in the world, including among its innovations such materials as cellophane, nylon and Kevlar®.

Panama Canal

## Another Famous Midnight Ride

IN 1776, THE DECLARATION of Independence came within one vote of not being ratified. On July 1, the Continental Congress was deadlocked, with two of Delaware's delegates splitting on the issue. A third delegate — Caesar Rodney — was at home contending with several state offices he held at the time. When word of the impasse arrived, Rodney dropped everything and mounted his horse. After riding alone overnight through a furious thunderstorm, Rodney burst into the Continental Congress during the last moments of debate, in time to cast the fateful vote for independence. At the time, Rodney was already suffering from the cancer that would claim his life shortly after the Revolutionary War — perhaps eclipsing the renown he might have earned as a leader in the fledgling nation that his midnight ride helped launch.

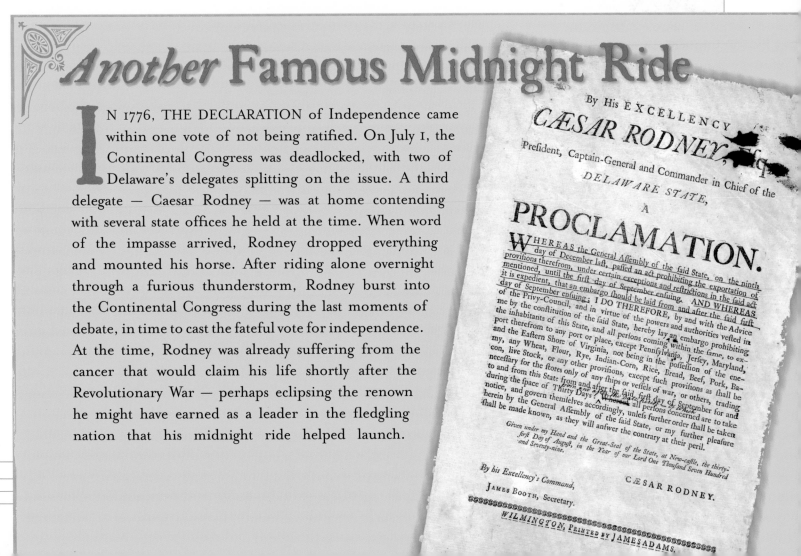

By His EXCELLENCY
CÆSAR RODNEY,
President, Captain-General and Commander in Chief of the
DELAWARE STATE,

A

## PROCLAMATION.

WHEREAS the General Assembly of the said State, on the ninth day of December last, passed an act prohibiting the exportation of provisions therefrom, under certain exceptions and restrictions in the said act mentioned, until the first day of September ensuing, AND WHEREAS it is expedient, that an embargo should be laid from and after the said first day of September ensuing; I DO THEREFORE, by and with the Advice of the Privy-Council, and in virtue of the powers and authorities vested in me by the constitution of the said State, hereby lay an embargo prohibiting the inhabitants of this State, and all persons coming within the same, to export therefrom to any port or place, except Pennsylvania, Jersey, Maryland, and the Eastern Shore of Virginia, not being in the possession of the enemy, any Wheat, Flour, Rye, Indian-Corn, Rice, Bread, Beef, Pork, Bacon, live Stock, or any other provisions, except such provisions as shall be necessary for the stores only of any ships or vessels of war, or others, trading to and from this State from and after the said first day of September for and during the space of Thirty Days; And all persons concerned are to take notice, and govern themselves accordingly, unless further order shall be taken herein by the General Assembly of the said State, or my further pleasure shall be made known, as they will answer the contrary at their peril.

Given under my Hand and the Great-Seal of the State, at New-castle, the thirty-first Day of August, in the Year of our Lord One Thousand Seven Hundred and Seventy-nine.

CÆSAR RODNEY.

By his Excellency's Command,
JAMES BOOTH, Secretary.

WILMINGTON, PRINTED BY JAMES ADAMS.

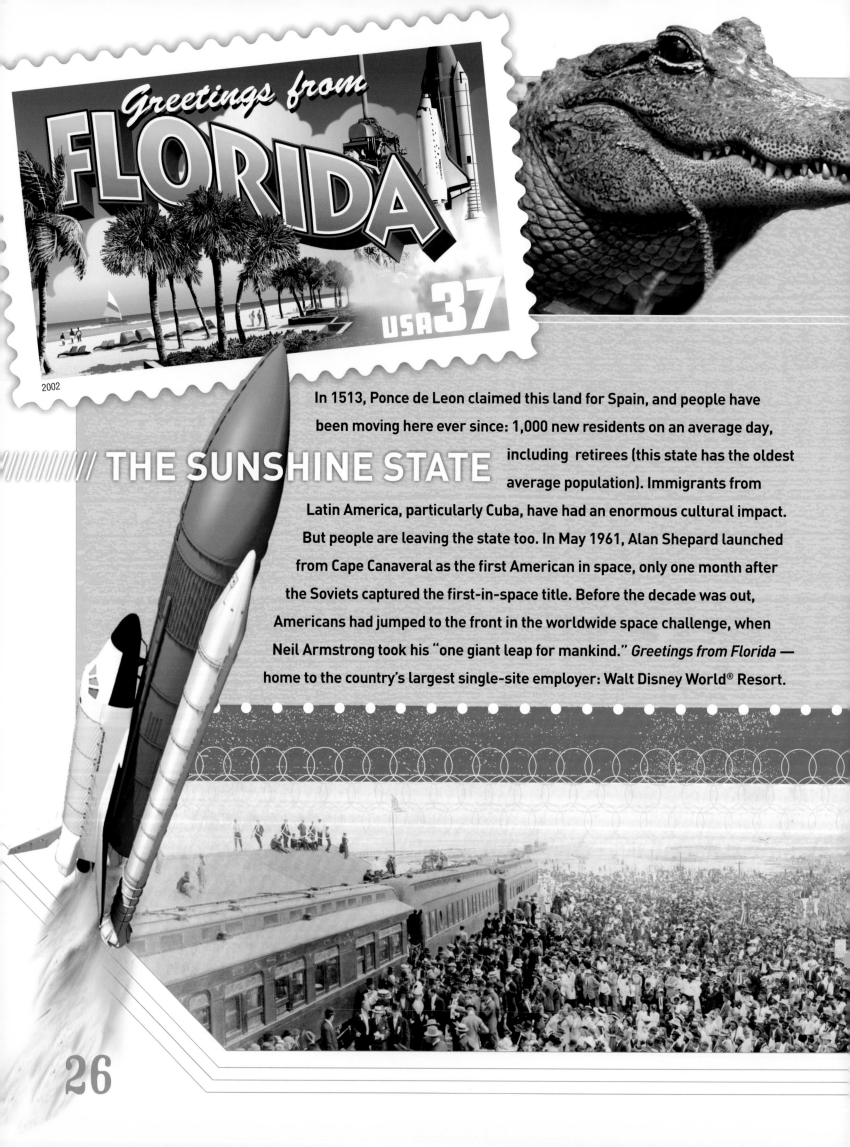

Greetings from **FLORIDA**

USA **37**

2002

///////////// THE SUNSHINE STATE

In 1513, Ponce de Leon claimed this land for Spain, and people have been moving here ever since: 1,000 new residents on an average day, including retirees (this state has the oldest average population). Immigrants from Latin America, particularly Cuba, have had an enormous cultural impact. But people are leaving the state too. In May 1961, Alan Shepard launched from Cape Canaveral as the first American in space, only one month after the Soviets captured the first-in-space title. Before the decade was out, Americans had jumped to the front in the worldwide space challenge, when Neil Armstrong took his "one giant leap for mankind." *Greetings from Florida* — home to the country's largest single-site employer: Walt Disney World® Resort.

PLEASE
NO SWIMMING !

# THE LAND NO ONE WANTED

MORE THAN TWO centuries ago, Florida was considered such a miserable swamp that Congress debated whether it was even worth acquiring from Spain. (Senator John Randolph of Virginia was adamantly opposed.) Since then, some detractors still point to the state's alligators, hurricanes and lightning strikes (the state holds the U.S. record for most fatalities caused by the electrical charges). Even so, many know that Florida has a lot to offer. Over the last 30 years, the state has grown at the rate of 3 million people per decade. After facing near-extinction in 1967, even the alligators are doing better.

NOT MANY PEOPLE WOULD DREAM OF building a railroad across 153 miles of mostly marshland and open water. Fewer still would have the $30 million needed to do so in the early 1900s. Perhaps, only one: Henry Flagler, one of the wealthiest men in America at the time. After retirement, he set about building his Florida Overseas Railway from Miami to Key West.

Newspapers dubbed it "Flagler's Folly," but Henry finished it. In 1912, after seven years of construction, he rode it proudly from end to end. Then, 23 years later, one of the state's infamous hurricanes destroyed it. The only remnants were a number of bridges, which later became the foundation for the Overseas Highway: the southernmost part of U.S. Highway 1, connecting the Florida Keys to the mainland.

FLAGLER'S FOLLY

Greetings from GEORGIA

37 USA

2002

## ////////// THE PEACH STATE

From the Okefenokee Swamp to the nation's first planned city (Savannah) to the first chartered, state-supported university (Go, Bulldogs!), Georgia is a state of contrast and contradiction. Its colonial charter guaranteed religious freedom — except for Roman Catholics. Its capital city elected an African-American mayor in 1973 — at the same time a Confederate battle flag flew over the Statehouse. While Georgia is a major producer of peaches, perhaps its nickname should be "the Vidalia® State," since it holds the exclusive rights to the name of that sweet onion.

Georgia also holds the record for the world's largest mass of exposed granite: Stone Mountain, home to the bas-relief sculpture of Confederate heroes Jefferson Davis, Robert E. Lee and Stonewall Jackson. The memorial is actually larger than Mount Rushmore. *Greetings from Georgia* — birthplace of Coca-Cola® and the Girl Scouts®.

28

# MENTOR
## *to Martin Luther King Jr.*

EACH JANUARY, THE NATION CELEBRATES the legacy of Martin Luther King Jr. Yet Dr. King's legacy is inextricably linked to that of Dr. Benjamin E. Mays — then-president of Atlanta's Morehouse College. When the two met, the future civil-rights leader was still a college student. Although the son and grandson of Baptist ministers, King didn't want to enter the ministry; he wanted to be a lawyer. But Mays' outspoken views against segregation and discrimination had a profound influence on King's life. In 1955, when King was helping to organize the Montgomery Bus Boycott in Alabama, he turned to Mays for direction. Dr. Mays urged King to continue working for a nonviolent solution to a boycott that eventually stretched out for more than a year. After King's assassination in 1968, it was Benjamin Mays who delivered the final eulogy from the Morehouse College chapel.

# Sherman's March

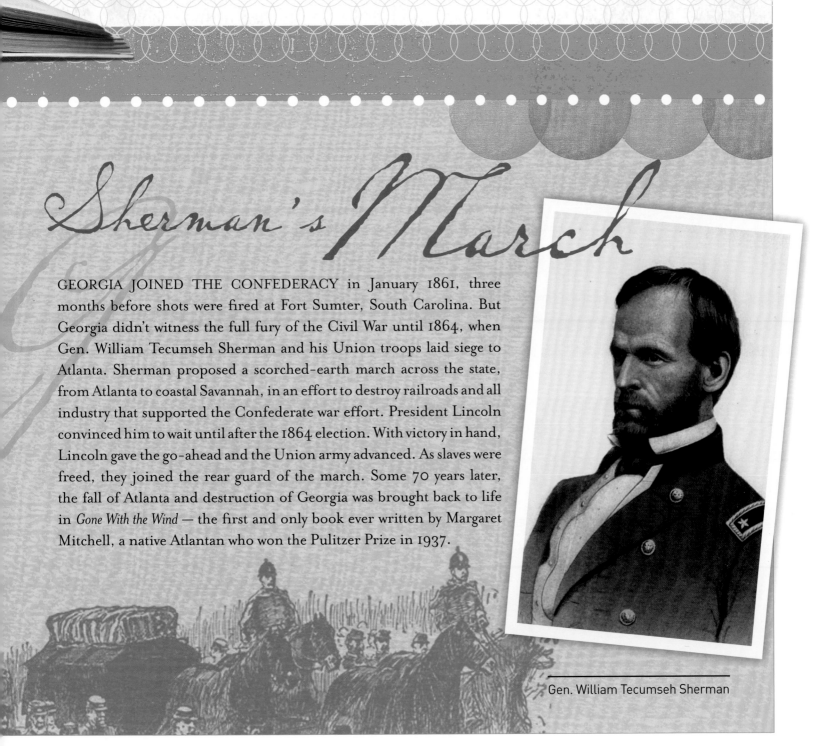

GEORGIA JOINED THE CONFEDERACY in January 1861, three months before shots were fired at Fort Sumter, South Carolina. But Georgia didn't witness the full fury of the Civil War until 1864, when Gen. William Tecumseh Sherman and his Union troops laid siege to Atlanta. Sherman proposed a scorched-earth march across the state, from Atlanta to coastal Savannah, in an effort to destroy railroads and all industry that supported the Confederate war effort. President Lincoln convinced him to wait until after the 1864 election. With victory in hand, Lincoln gave the go-ahead and the Union army advanced. As slaves were freed, they joined the rear guard of the march. Some 70 years later, the fall of Atlanta and destruction of Georgia was brought back to life in *Gone With the Wind* — the first and only book ever written by Margaret Mitchell, a native Atlantan who won the Pulitzer Prize in 1937.

Gen. William Tecumseh Sherman

37 USA

2002

*Greetings*
FROM
**HAWAII**

///////////// **THE ALOHA STATE** How many states host lava flows, coffee farms and one of the largest cattle ranches in the United States? Hawaii enjoys other unique features, as well as a native language with the world's second-shortest alphabet — only 12 letters. Hawaii is also the most isolated major population center on earth, located almost 2,400 miles from California and more than 3,800 miles from Japan.

Some of Hawaii's unique traditions, however, were nearly lost to Western influences. In the early 1900s, Duke Kahanamoku began reviving one of them: surfing the beaches of Oahu using a towering, solid-wood board. His success put surfing in the international spotlight and helped to preserve this ancient Hawaiian sport. Duke also won three gold medals and two silvers as a member of the U.S. Olympic Swimming team and was inducted into the U.S. Olympic Hall of Fame.

*Greetings from Hawaii* — home to thousands of orchid varieties and America's only royal palace.

# The Kingdom of Hawaii

THE HAWAIIAN ISLANDS were ruled by feudal chieftains and remained isolated from the Western world until 1778, when English navigator James Cook arrived. He named them the Sandwich Islands after one of his sponsors, the fourth Earl of Sandwich. In 1810, the islands were unified into one kingdom under the great King Kamehameha I.

Hawaii was recognized as an independent, constitutional monarchy until its sovereignty began to be threatened by tycoons, plantation owners and others with strong interests in annexation. Finally, in 1893, Hawaii's Queen Liliuokalani was deposed in a bloodless coup with the help of U.S. Marines dispatched from the *USS Boston*. Not all Hawaiians embraced this new democracy, but after various revolts and provisional governments, the United States annexed the islands in 1898. Hawaii joined the union as the 50th state on August 21, 1959.

# HAWAIIAN HEROES

AFTER ANNEXATION, Hawaii's strategic position in the South Pacific made it ideal for an American military base. It also made it an ideal target. The Japanese attacked Pearl Harbor on December 7, 1941, catapulting America into World War II. Japanese Americans living in Hawaii and on the U.S. mainland became subject to harassment and internment. At the same time, their sons were enlisting in the Army. The 100th Infantry Battalion and the 442nd Regimental Combat Team were composed almost entirely of Japanese Americans, the majority from Hawaii. The combined 100th/442nd emerged as the most decorated unit of its size in American history, with more than 18,000 medals, citations and awards. Yet they paid a high price: An unprecedented casualty rate earned them the nickname the "Purple Heart Battalion." Their astonishing war record gained them the respect they had long been denied.

# //////// THE GEM STATE

Wilderness lovers, look no further. With 30 state parks and 13 national forests within its borders, Idaho offers plenty for those who love the outdoors. The country's highest falls aren't Niagara, they're Idaho's Shoshone Falls. The deepest gorge is not the Grand Canyon. It's Hell's Canyon, on the Oregon-Idaho border. With 93,000 miles of rivers and streams, and an almost unparalleled collection of eagles, hawks and falcons, it's no wonder that this state is a Mecca for anglers and hikers from all around the country. *Greetings from Idaho* — home of the cutthroat trout.

2002

32

# The SPUD STATE

INCREASING NUMBERS IN UTAH'S SALT LAKE VALLEY sent Mormon pioneers elsewhere, some settling in 1860 in what they thought was northern Utah. A later survey determined that they had crossed into Idaho. They had good fortune planting potatoes — and the rest is history.

But we have more than Mormon settlers to thank for our french fries. Idaho's Jack Simplot perfected a method for making processed frozen potatoes. Today, the J.R. Simplot® Company produces about 3 billion pounds of french fries and other potato products per year. Blackfoot's Idaho Potato Expo (slogan: "Free Taters for Out-of-Staters") lays claim to the World's Largest Baked Potato. But put your forks away — inside, it's mostly chicken wire and stuffing.

Thanks to one of the most successful commodity marketing campaigns in history, when we think of Idaho, we think, *potatoes*. And though Idaho leads the nation in potato production, less than 20 percent of Idaho's total economy comes from agriculture.

# A SILVER LINING

MOST OF IDAHO'S AGRICULTURE thrives in the southern part of the state, while the roots of the narrow north belong to mining. Perhaps 20,000 of the famed "Forty-Niners" passed through Idaho en route to California gold. Eleven years later, many would return for Idaho's own gold rush. Elias Pierce found gold in Clearwater County in 1860 and established Pierce, Idaho — the state's oldest mining community. Idaho's mining boom began with gold, but soon, entrepreneurial gold prospectors were replaced by corporations pursuing the state's abundance of lead, copper, zinc and silver. Northern Idaho's aptly named Silver Valley produced more than a billion ounces of silver between 1884 and 2005. Today, Idaho ranks third in U.S. silver production.

## //////// THE PRAIRIE STATE

Urban and rural, modern and grounded in the past, Illinois is "Middle America" in almost every sense of the term. Home of the tallest building in North America — Chicago's Sears Tower — Illinois also has some of the most productive farmland in the world.

And Illinois is celebrated as the home, although not the birthplace, of Abraham Lincoln. A political rivalry in 1842 left Lincoln at odds with James Shields, who was state auditor when Lincoln was a state representative. When a letter to the editor offended Shields, he accused Lincoln of writing the letter and challenged him to a duel. As the challenged party, Lincoln had the choice of weapons. He chose broadswords, ensuring the much taller Lincoln an insurmountable advantage. Eventually, the men agreed to forgo the duel. In the end, the two became close friends. *Greetings from Illinois* — the land of Lincoln.

Abraham Lincoln

# The Great Pyramids of Illinois

ILLINOIS' ANCIENT CITY OF CAHOKIA represents a lost civilization and an enduring mystery. Believed to be the largest city built north of Mexico before the arrival of Columbus, the once-booming Cahokia was abandoned about a century before European settlement began. Even the name is a misnomer: "Cahokia" identifies the people who settled there centuries after the ancient city's decline. The original civilization left no written record but is remembered now for its pyramids, which rival ancient Egypt's. The largest surviving pyramid, Monk's Mound, covers 14 acres. Estimates suggest that construction required more than 14 million baskets of soil, all carried by human workers. No one knows for sure why Cahokia was abandoned. Some suggest that the city's growth depleted local resources, causing the population to shrink and, eventually, vanish.

# Scarface

HE GREW UP IN NEW YORK, but his escapades made Al Capone the most infamous Chicagoan of his era. Capone built a criminal empire by supplying what Prohibition had made illegal — alcohol — as well as the unlawful pastimes of gambling and prostitution.

Capone's celebrity soured on Valentine's Day 1929. In an elaborate plot aimed at a rival gang, bootleggers were lured to a meeting place to buy high-quality whiskey at an attractive price. Capone's men posed as policemen, apprehending the gang during the transaction. Caught in the act, the bootleggers did what they were told and lined up against a wall. Then Capone's gang opened fire, gunning down seven men. When police arrived at the scene of the massacre, they found one man barely alive, claiming he had not been shot — despite 22 bullet wounds.

The brazen crime stirred President Herbert Hoover to devote the resources of the federal government to putting Capone behind bars. In 1931, Al Capone was convicted and sentenced — for tax evasion.

## AL CAPONE

2002

## ///////// THE HOOSIER STATE

Indiana's limestone is treasured as a top-quality building material, used in major cities across America and in such celebrated venues as the Empire State Building and the Pentagon. The term "Hoosier" is thought to be derived from the Anglo-Saxon term for "hill." So a Hoosier is a hill-dweller, a term celebrating Indiana's rough-hewn pioneers. Territorial governor William Henry ("Old Tippecanoe") Harrison embodied the Indiana pioneer. His exploits in battle would drive him to the White House. Yet Harrison's frontier spirit did him no favors on a cold, wet Inauguration Day in 1841. He refused to wear an overcoat or hat as he gave the longest Inauguration speech in history. Harrison then developed pneumonia and died a month later — the first American president to die in office. *Greetings from Indiana* — where the presidential slogan "Tippecanoe and Tyler Too" became a household phrase.

William Henry Harrison

# WANTED

## PUBLIC ENEMY № 1

IN THE 1930S, banks were not widely popular, better known for the foreclosures that became common during the Great Depression. So John Dillinger's 14-month bank-robbing spree captured the imagination of the entire country.

The FBI's inability to capture Dillinger became a major embarrassment to Director J. Edgar Hoover. But Dillinger's end came at the hands of FBI agents, thanks to a girlfriend-turned-informant. Dillinger died in a gun battle with agents outside Chicago's Biograph Theater on July 22, 1934. Yet when his body was returned to his hometown for burial, some locals claimed it wasn't their boy, adding to the legend of Indiana's most famous master criminal.

## $10,000.<sup>00</sup>

## THE ORIGINAL
## Motor City

ALTHOUGH DETROIT, MICHIGAN, is widely regarded as the home of the American automobile industry, the car business actually got its start in Indianapolis. In 1909, the city's many carmakers found Indiana's old-fashioned wagon roads a risky place to test their products. So four businessmen decided to build a track to test and show off local manufacturers' faster, more powerful cars. The track's original surface of crushed rock and tar soon gave way to paving bricks, a surface that still lies under today's asphalt at the Indianapolis Motor Speedway®.

In 1911, spectators were invited to witness an endurance test — and the Indianapolis 500 was born. Ray Harroun won that first race, driving his Marmon Wasp to an average speed of 75 mph. In the early 1900s, Indiana produced almost 200 different automobile models, with names such as the Union, the Nyberg and the De Tamble. Today, the "motor city" mantle has moved to Detroit, yet the Indianapolis 500 is still regarded as the largest single-day sporting event in the world.

# THE HAWKEYE STATE

Welcome to a state whose nickname was inspired by a character in the classic book *The Last of the Mohicans*. Iowa is the only state whose full eastern and western borders are rivers. In between, an ancient glacier formed some of the most fertile soil in the world, making Iowa the biggest corn producer in the United States — and corn means a lot of things.

A family today could cross Iowa driving with fuel enriched by Iowa corn — while drinking a soft drink sweetened with Iowa corn. Perhaps, some of the plastic in their car would be derived from Iowa corn stalks. During the journey, the family might stop for dinner and enjoy some . . . well, it turns out you can eat the stuff too.

*Greetings from Iowa* — birthplace of the Winnebago®, named for a well-traveled Indian tribe.

Greetings FROM IOWA

USA 37

2002

# The Iowa Caucuses

IOWANS ARE CELEBRATED for their common sense, right down to the way they govern themselves. Iowa's 99 counties consist of self-governing townships, so Iowa's neighbors have always worked together at election time. But in the age of television, Iowa has become an American political phenomenon.

In 1976, Jimmy Carter actually finished second in the Iowa caucuses — behind "undecided." Still, he was able to parlay that "win" into a political run that ended in the White House. And ever since, it has been each Iowan's birthright to interrogate the next would-be president of the United States.

After extended political polling and punditry, the Iowa caucuses traditionally represent the first statewide, binding, public expression of candidate preference. New Hampshire and a host of other states follow shortly after with their primaries, but every four years the presidential political season officially begins in a way that is uniquely American — and distinctly Iowan.

## Race across the state

DURING THE LAST WEEK OF EVERY JULY since 1973, thousands of bike riders have completed a route nearly from coast to coast. Iowa's coasts, that is. Called RAGBRAI® — "Register's Annual Great Bicycle Ride Across Iowa" — the tradition began as a trek by two writers for *The Des Moines Register*, now the primary sponsor of the event.

The ride's route changes annually but always proceeds from near the state's western border to the Mississippi River in the east. Through the years, RAGBRAI has passed through more than 750 Iowa towns.

Up to 8,500 riders participate in the weeklong event. In 2006, his first year after retiring from Tour de France™ competition, Lance Armstrong participated in RAGBRAI. He announced plans to bring 150 riders to the event in 2007.

## THE SUNFLOWER STATE

When Dorothy was whisked away from her prairie homeland to the Land of Oz, it was courtesy of a giant Kansas twister. Kansas resides in "Tornado Alley" — a narrow strip of central states that receive most of the country's estimated 1,000 tornadoes each year. In fact, tornadoes hit the small town of Codell on May 20, three years in a row, in 1916, 1917 and 1918. But Kansas weather isn't always stormy. An average year sees more than 225 sunny days, thus cultivating sunflowers and the state's nickname.

Sunny days are good for flying, and that's important in Wichita, which is a major manufacturing center for Cessna℠, Boeing®, Beech℠ and Learjet™, making it the "Air Capital of the World." Wichita was home for the production of the B-29 Superfortress — the bomber that helped win World War II.

*Greetings from Kansas* — birthplace of Amelia Earhart.

# DODGE CITY

FORT DODGE WAS ESTABLISHED IN 1865 on the Santa Fe Trail as protection for wagon trains and as a supply base for troops during the Indian Wars. In 1872, a fledgling frontier town named Dodge City sprang up nearby and became a center for the buffalo trade. When hunting began to decimate the buffalo herds, Longhorn cattle from Texas took their place. The cattle were driven into Dodge City and shipped to bigger cities by train. At its peak, the railroad loaded as many as 500,000 head of cattle a year at Dodge City. When Kansas imposed quarantines on Texas Longhorns in 1885 to protect local herds from disease, the great era of cattle drives and cowboys came to an end.

## Bleeding KANSAS

IN 1854, THE PASSAGE OF THE KANSAS-NEBRASKA ACT allowed people in those two new territories to decide whether or not to allow slavery. The act repealed the 1820 Missouri Compromise, which would have outlawed slavery in both territories. Pro- and anti-slavery forces rushed in, hoping to affect the first elections after the act's passage. Numerous violent events ensued, earning the state the nickname "Bleeding Kansas."

In May 1856, pro-slavery militia attacked the city of Lawrence. In retaliation, abolitionist John Brown killed five pro-slavery settlers living along Pottawotomie Creek. Brown ultimately fled Kansas and went on to lead the failed 1859 slave revolt at Harper's Ferry, in modern-day West Virginia, for which he was executed. In 1861, Kansas was admitted to the Union as a free state.

## THE BLUEGRASS STATE

The grass isn't really blue here. It's just that the spring buds have a bluish cast to them. Still, the name has stuck. Fewer people know that Kentucky is the only state with a small parcel of land, known as Kentucky Bend, that's completely surrounded by other states. This area is located within a hairpin turn of the Mississippi River that was created when a series of earthquakes in the early 1800s changed the river's course.

The Kentucky-West Virginia backcountry was also home to the infamous feud between the Hatfields and the McCoys, which lasted more than a decade in the late 1800s and eventually involved both the National Guard and the U.S. Supreme Court.

Perhaps the habit of feuding is part of Kentucky's character: During the Civil War, Kentucky had competing North/South factions and was a slave-holding state, but it declared itself neutral in May 1861. President Abraham Lincoln and Confederate President Jefferson Davis were both born in Kentucky, just one year apart. Baseball, however, is a Kentucky pastime that unites everyone. *Greetings from Kentucky* — home of the Louisville Slugger®.

# The Kentucky Derby

IN 1872, PROMINENT LOUISVILLE CITIZEN Meriwether Lewis Clark Jr. (grandson of William Clark, of the famed Lewis and Clark exploring team), traveled from Kentucky to England and France, to study racing there. Upon returning home, Clark helped form the Louisville Jockey Club to raise money to build a racing facility in Kentucky. The first derby was held in 1875 with a field of 3-year-old horses and an estimated crowd of 10,000 spectators. Fourteen of the 15 jockeys in the race, including the winner, were African Americans. Today, the Kentucky Derby is a $2 million race that attracts crowds of more than 150,000 each year. It's also the oldest consecutively held thoroughbred horse race in America and the first race in the country's Triple Crown.

# FAMOUS FRONTIERSMAN

DANIEL BOONE'S FRONTIER EXPLOITS made him one of America's first folk heroes. In 1775, after blazing the Wilderness Road west through the Appalachian Mountains, he established the town of Boonesborough. His published exploits, *Adventures*, helped establish Boone as a legend. The Kentucky Historical Society even celebrates June 7 as "Boone Day," commemorating the day in 1769 when the pioneer first saw Kentucky land. In the 1826 classic *The Last of the Mohicans*, James Fenimore Cooper penned a dramatic scene likely based on Boone's life: In 1776, Boone rescued his daughter and two other teenage girls after they were captured by a Shawnee Indian war party. Boone eventually traveled even farther west, to Missouri, where he lived until his death in 1820. Sometime later, the remains of Boone and his wife were returned to rest in Kentucky.

Daniel Boone

# //////////// THE PELICAN STATE

Water has always played a crucial role in this state, from the Gulf and the many bayous, to numerous lakes and waterways, to the mighty Mississippi River. With all that water underfoot, Louisiana boasts a lot of bridges. The Lake Pontchartrain Causeway — at just short of 24 miles — is the longest water bridge in the world.

Although the Spanish were the first Europeans to arrive in the region that would become Louisiana, French explorer Robert Cavelier de la Salle claimed the entire Mississippi Basin for France in 1682. But the state owes much of its French heritage to settlers from Canada. In 1755, a portion of the French-speaking population of Acadia (now Nova Scotia) was expelled at gunpoint by the British, who feared a future alliance with France. Some eventually immigrated to Louisiana, where the name used to describe them — *Acadian* — was later shortened to *Cajun*. In 1803, France sold the region to the United States as part of the Louisiana Purchase. *Greetings from Louisiana* — named after King Louis XIV of France.

2002

44

Andrew Jackson

# THE BATTLE OF ★★★★
# *New Orleans*

LOUISIANANS CELEBRATE the Fourth of July — Independence Day — but they consider January 8 to be nearly as important. That day marks the 1815 victory of the Battle of New Orleans, a skirmish that actually occurred after the War of 1812 had already ended. Major General Andrew Jackson led a poorly equipped, small army that included pirates, Choctaw Indians and free blacks against some 8,000 British troops. The Americans prevailed and Jackson became a national hero. With the unprecedented victory, Jackson saved New Orleans as well as control of the river and was catapulted into the presidency in 1829. New Orleans was the site for another battle in 1862, when federal troops captured it after Louisiana's secession, thus controlling the gateway to the Mississippi River and the entire river valley.

# THE GREAT FLOOD of 1927

HURRICANE KATRINA is considered the most devastating and costly natural disaster in U.S. history, yet it was not without precedent. Beginning in summer 1926, rainfall over the entire Mississippi River Valley began setting all-time records. By spring 1927, portions of seven states were under water. In Louisiana, the flooding displaced an estimated 700,000 people. A decision by the U.S. Army Corps of Engineers — to blast the levee at a point downriver from New Orleans, sending the water into marshland — is credited with saving the city. The poor suffered greatly in the devastation, and their biggest advocate was Governor Huey P. Long and his later reforms. Long was perhaps best known for his "Share Our Wealth" movement, which advocated redistributing the nation's wealth among the people. Many believed Long would run for president in 1936, against Franklin Delano Roosevelt, but an assassin's bullet cut short his political ambitions and his life in 1935.

## THE PINE TREE STATE

Maine is nearly as large as the other five New England states combined, with a dramatic terrain that includes more than 5,000 coastal islands and forests covering 90 percent of its land. That explains why this state is America's second-leading paper producer and also churns out 90 percent of the country's wooden toothpicks. Maine's coastline includes more than 60 picturesque lighthouses as well as a delicacy for which the state is perhaps best known: lobster. In Colonial times, lobster was regarded as fit only for prisoners and indentured servants. But today, Maine's lobstermen catch more than 50 million pounds of this coveted crustacean each year.

Apart from its lobster fame, Maine was also inches away from being the site of the first permanent English settlement in New England. Instead, the harsh weather drove settlers from Popham Colony, established in 1607. *Greetings from Maine* — the largest blueberry producer in the world.

46

# THE RUM RIOT

IN 1851, PORTLAND'S MAYOR, NEAL DOW, championed a controversial Prohibition law. The so-called Maine Law stood as a crucial victory for the temperance movement, with Maine becoming the first state to prohibit the manufacture and sale of alcoholic beverages, except for medicinal or mechanical purposes. In June 1855, opposition to the law turned violent when word spread that a supply of medicinal alcohol was being stored in the basement of City Hall. A group of more than 3,000 stormed City Hall, and Dow called out the militia. The ensuing riot left one person dead and many wounded, and effectively ended Dow's local political career. He volunteered for the military instead and carried his temperance convictions with him into the 13th Maine Volunteer Infantry Regiment. Dow later ran as the candidate for president of the United States on the Prohibition ticket in 1880.

CLOSE THE SALOONS

IF you believe that the traffic in alcohol does more harm than good — Help stop it.

# L.L.BEAN®

ANOTHER MAINER MADE HIS MARK on the world in 1912, when he invented a boot that would keep his feet dry while hunting. Leon Leonwood Bean soon realized that the boot was popular with his friends as well, so he decided to start making more and selling them. The original L.L.Bean catalog was actually a simple flier featuring one product only: L.L.'s Maine Hunting shoe. Over the years, the catalog has expanded far beyond the boot, but visitors can still watch craftsmen make that signature boot the old-fashioned way: by hand. The store — in the town of Freeport — has no locks and is open 24 hours a day, seven days a week, 365 days a year.

Leon Leonwood Bean

2002

## ////////// THE OLD LINE STATE

Maryland is widely regarded as the home of Babe Ruth, Chesapeake Bay crabs, and the dividing line between the North and the South. Lesser known is the fact that Maryland was the first Catholic colony in North America and home to the country's first Catholic cathedral: the Baltimore Basilica.

Maryland's official team sport is lacrosse, which originated with Native Americans, but it's baseball that opens its games with "The Star Spangled Banner." Francis Scott Key wrote the U.S. national anthem in 1814, to memorialize the survival of Baltimore's Fort McHenry — and the American flag — following a British bombardment.

*Greetings from Maryland* — believed to be nicknamed by George Washington himself in recognition of his brave, regular-line troops during the Revolutionary War.

Francis Scott Key

# A State Divided

DESPITE THE PRESENCE of the Mason-Dixon Line between Maryland and Pennsylvania, Maryland was officially a Northern state. The Mason-Dixon Line actually predates the Civil War and was established in the 1760s after a property dispute. The two who surveyed the boundary were Englishmen Charles Mason and Jeremiah Dixon.

Although Maryland never seceded from the Union, the first official bloodshed of the Civil War occurred in Baltimore in April 1861, when Maryland's Confederate sympathizers attacked Union soldiers traveling through on their way to protect Washington. Many Marylanders viewed the federal troops as an invading army and attacked; terrified soldiers fired back; and President Lincoln soon declared martial law. Federal officers arrested the mayor, police chief and several others, transporting them to Fort McHenry. Maryland remained a state divided by loyalties throughout the war.

# DISTRICT of COLUMBIA

WITHIN THE BORDERS OF MARYLAND lies a unique tract of land — 61 square miles — ceded from the state to the nation. Many of America's most powerful decisions are made in this area that possesses federal status without any states' rights: the District of Columbia. The district is represented by one member of Congress, who carries the responsibilities of office and can vote in committees but lacks the right to vote on the House floor. Over the years, various plans have been put forth to allow D.C. citizens a voice in Congress without becoming a separate state. It's even been suggested that the city be given back to Maryland — so far, that idea has received little support. For now, the state and the district remain separate entities, joined together in spirit by a common heritage and history.

# //////////// THE BAY STATE

Old states contain many firsts. Massachusetts, one of the original 13 colonies, is home to the first U.S. subway system, the oldest U. S. institution of higher learning and the first basketball game. The first nuclear-powered surface vessel was built here, and four U.S. presidents were born here — all in the same county. The Adams and Bush families are among eight U.S. presidential families known to have descended from passengers of the Mayflower — the ship that carried the Pilgrims to our shoreline to found the Plymouth Colony in 1620. A decade later, the Puritans arrived, seeking to escape religious persecution. The bloody Pequot War followed soon after — the first of many wars between Native Americans and English settlers seeking to assert dominance. *Greetings from Massachusetts* — home of the country's oldest major-league ballpark still in operation, Fenway Park.

GREETINGS FROM MASSACHUSETTS

USA 37

2002

# THE GLOUCESTERMEN

UST NORTH OF Boston lies the seaside town of Gloucester, renowned for its maritime traditions. Gloucester was America's first major fishing port, as well as an important shipbuilding center. In 1713, shipbuilder Andrew Robinson launched a new type of ship from here: the schooner. And over the next three centuries, thousands of fishermen lost their lives after sailing from these shores. In 1925, a bronze fisherman took up residence overlooking Gloucester's harbor — a statue dedicated to "they that go down to the sea in ships." In 2001, the Gloucester Fishermen's Wives Association dedicated another monument overlooking the harbor — one honoring the women who have long waited for their husbands to return.

## Statue of Three Lies

AS RELIGIOUS DISSENTERS in England, young Puritan ministers were forced to sign an act of conformity to the Anglican Church if they desired a degree from Oxford or Cambridge. So, once they reached the New World, they created a new university: Harvard. On the campus today stands a statue bearing the inscription, *John Harvard, founder, 1638.* The monument is also known as "The Statue of Three Lies," because the statue was not modeled after John Harvard (there were no known likenesses of him); he was not the founder of Harvard (rather, the school was named after him); and the school was founded in 1636, not 1638.

Greetings *from* MICHIGAN

37 USA

2002

## //////// THE GREAT LAKE STATE

This unique state has the largest freshwater shoreline in the world, because it's encircled by four of the five Great Lakes. With those large, well-traveled bodies of water, it's no surprise that Michigan has over 120 lighthouses — more than any other state. Most people know Michigan as home to the American auto industry. Indeed, Henry Ford's River Rouge Complex was an amazing multiplex of 93 buildings and its own railroad, with at least 90 miles of track.

One former autoworker went into another field entirely, forming Motown[SM] Records in 1959. Berry Gordy's family had moved to Michigan from Georgia in 1922, as part of the Great Migration — when more than a million African Americans relocated from south to north. *Greetings from Michigan* — home of brothers John and Will Kellogg, who invented corn flakes.

# TIMBER. Green Gold

IN THE 19TH CENTURY, Michigan's vast expanse of old-growth white pines — and the abundance of rivers with which to transport the timber — seemed to promise endless prosperity. By the late 1800s, Michigan was the leading producer of lumber in the entire United States. By the early 20th century, however, Michigan's forests had been over-harvested. The passing of the 1903 Forest Reserve Act initiated reforestation of the state, and now Michigan has the largest state-forest system in the United States, managing almost 4 million acres. In 1955, the eastern white pine was designated the state tree.

# Detroit-Windsor
# TUNNEL

THE GREAT LAKES and their tributary rivers support an extensive wildlife habitat and form a natural, 721-mile boundary between Michigan and its international neighbor, Ontario, Canada. For many years, ferries offered the only way to cross the Detroit River between the two countries. But the growth of the car industry after World War I overburdened the ferry system's capacity.

The solution was the nearly mile-long Detroit-Windsor Tunnel, an unparalleled engineering feat that opened in November 1930. It was the first vehicular sub-aquatic tunnel built between two nations. Every day, more than 27,000 vehicles use the tunnel — one of the busiest border-crossing points between the United States and Canada.

Detroit-Windsor Tunnel construction crew

37 USA

Greetings from

MINNESOTA

2002

# THE NORTH STAR STATE

This state is cold — very cold. In fact, its lowest recorded temperature was minus 60 degrees, in 1996. But frosty temperatures can foster creativity. For example, the roof of the climate-controlled Metrodome is covered by more than 10 acres of Teflon®-coated, fiberglass, which needs 250,000 cubic feet of air pressure per minute to stay inflated. The chilly weather also inspired the nation's first enclosed shopping mall and Minneapolis' famed Skyway System — more than 8 miles of enclosed walkways. Then, of course, there's the Mall of America®, which boasts its own police station, post office, church and indoor amusement park — all enjoyed by more than 40 million visitors a year. *Greetings from Minnesota* — home of Garrison Keillor's "A Prairie Home Companion®" and the radio show's fictional town of Lake Wobegon℠.

The cast of "A Prairie Home Companion"

# *Northwest* ANGLE

FOR A HANDFUL of Minnesotans today, home is so far north that it's actually in Canada — the northernmost part of the contiguous United States. Known as the Northwest Angle, this geographic anomaly is the result of a mapping error made after the American Revolution. The Angle can only be reached from the Canadian provinces of Manitoba and Ontario, or by water. As of the 2000 census, 152 Minnesotans lived year-round on the Angle, which juts out into Lake of the Woods. The Angle made history in 1998 when a group of residents announced their desire to secede from the United States and join Manitoba, citing fishing-rights disputes.

# TACONITE

IN AN AREA OF NORTHEAST Minnesota known as the Mesabi Range, the term "black gold" means ore, not oil. These iron ore veins were discovered in the late 19th century but were almost exhausted by the 1950s. Then, a team at the University of Minnesota developed a technique that extracts ore from lower-grade rock called taconite, which was previously discarded as waste but contains at least 25-percent iron. Since 2000, the Mesabi Range taconite mines have provided two-thirds of the iron used to build American cars, ships, homes and bridges.

# THE MAGNOLIA STATE

This Bible Belt state boasts not only the nation's largest Bible-binding plant but also creative talents such as the King of Rock and Roll. Nearly 100,000 visitors a year travel to Tupelo, birthplace of Elvis Presley, to see his modest, two-room house and adjacent museum and chapel.

In the late 19th century, former slaves and their descendents in this state combined work chants, gospel music and inspiration from their own hard times to create a unique form of music original to America: the blues. Mississippi musicians such as Howlin' Wolf and Muddy Waters spread the blues up the river to Memphis, St. Louis and, eventually, Chicago. The Ground Zero Blues Club℠ and Delta Blues Museum℠ are doing their part to ensure that the legacy of Mississippi blues is kept alive.

*Greetings from Mississippi* — home to the International Checker Hall of Fame.

GREETINGS FROM MISSISSIPPI

37 USA

2002

Battle of Vicksburg

56

# KING COTTON

COTTON HAS LONG BEEN GROWN across the South, but the laborious task of picking out seeds by hand once limited the quantity that could be turned into cloth. Tobacco was the greater cash crop. Things changed with the invention of the cotton gin in 1793, combined with the discovery of fertile soil and ideal weather in the newly organized Mississippi Territory. The booming textile industry in the northern states and in Europe soon created an unprecedented demand for cotton in the 19th century. Mississippi's economy became dependent upon slavery to plant and harvest the crop, despite nationwide cries for abolition and the start of the Civil War. In May 1861, the Confederate Congress prohibited the sale of cotton to the North, yet illicit trade still existed across enemy lines. Today, agriculture is the state's No. 1 industry, and cotton continues to play an important role.

## Reconstruction HEROES

THE POST CIVIL WAR RECONSTRUCTION EFFORT HIT full stride when Mississippi elected the first two African-American senators in U.S. history: Hiram Revels and Blanche Kelso Bruce. Born a free man in North Carolina in the 1820s, Revels was later ordained a minister and served as Union chaplain of a Mississippi regiment of free blacks. He then was elected to fill the empty Senate seat of former Confederate President Jefferson Davis, as Mississippi prepared to rejoin the Union. Bruce was born into slavery in 1841 and later tutored alongside his master's son. During the Civil War he escaped and went west. After the war, Bruce moved to Mississippi and acquired land; he then held various political posts until his election. Bruce became the first African American to serve a full term in the U.S. Senate — 1875 to 1881 — and pressed for civil rights for African Americans, Native Americans, Chinese immigrants and even former Confederates.

## ////////// THE SHOW ME STATE

Politics is something Missouri folks know a thing or two about. In all but one presidential election since 1900, the state has picked the winner (Missourians voted for Adlai Stevenson in 1956). Kansas City, one of the state's two major metropolitan areas, has been nicknamed by some as the "City of Fountains," for its 200 registered fountains. To the east, St. Louis is home to the country's tallest man-made monument: the Gateway Arch, built to commemorate Missouri's pivotal role in America's westward expansion. Riverboats played a major part in that expansion, and one of the country's most famous riverboat captains was Missouri's own Samuel Clemens, better known as Mark Twain.

*Greetings from Missouri* — known for its stalwart, sometimes stubborn attitude ("You've got to show me!") and which showed *itself* to the world when it hosted the first Olympic Games held in the United States, in 1904.

# the shape of the state

MISSOURI, LIKE MANY OF THE WESTERN STATES, started out as part of something bigger. In this case, it was the 1803 Louisiana Purchase. The region that would become Missouri experienced several defining boundary changes. In winter 1811-1812, the town of New Madrid was rocked by several powerful earthquakes — the largest ever recorded in the lower 48 states. The earthquakes effectively changed the course of the Mississippi River, which defined Missouri's eastern boundary. A landowner named John Walker snatched up some of the land and later lobbied to have his holdings added to the soon-to-become state. It was Walker's annexed land, in the southeast corner, that gave Missouri its distinctive "bootheel." In 1836, the state's shape changed again, after William Clark — of Lewis and Clark exploring fame — signed a treaty with local Indians. He paid them $7,500 to relinquish land and move farther west.

# Missouri Beverages

AMONG MISSOURI'S EARLY immigrants were French and German settlers who invested their talents to make the state a world leader in — believe it or not — wine making. In the mid-1880s, Missouri's hybrid vines were even shipped to France — just in time to graft into the French crop, which had been devastated by a pest to which their grapes had no resistance.

Prohibition laws dealt a severe blow to Missouri and its more than 100 wineries; the industry has been rebuilding ever since. Prohibition also dealt a blow to another famous Missouri beverage. In the 1860s, German immigrants Adolphus Busch and Eberhard Anheuser set out to revolutionize the beer industry, eventually pioneering that industry's use of refrigerated railcars and pasteurization.

During Prohibition, Anheuser-Busch® survived by making cheap products such as baking yeast and ice cream. With the repeal of Prohibition, Anheuser-Busch delivered a special gift to President Franklin D. Roosevelt: a case of cold ones, carried in by none other than a team of Clydesdales.

Greetings from *MONTANA*

USA**37**

2002

//////////// **THE TREASURE STATE**
There's plenty of room here in Big Sky Country — with not quite seven people for each of its 145,000-plus square miles. Plenty of room for Malmstrom Air Force Base and its 200 concrete silos that house ballistic missiles. Room, too, for the 50,000 or so spectators who gather each summer for Evel Knievel® Days — to meet and celebrate the homegrown daredevil. The sky seems to have a lot of room for unidentified flying objects. In fact, some call Montana the UFO capital of the United States. (Although Roswell, N.M., among other cities, might care to dispute that.) One reported UFO sighting, in Great Falls in 1950, was captured on 16 mm color film and submitted to the Air Force for review. When the film was returned to its owner, baseball manager Nicolas Mariana, he claimed that some footage was missing. *Greetings from Montana* — known for its rich mineral reserves.

# LITTLE BIG HORN

SEVERAL NORTHERN PLAINS Indian tribes, including the Cheyenne and Lakota Sioux, used to call Montana home. But American settlement conflicted with the treaty-reservation system and resulted in skirmishes between Indians and settlers. After entrepreneurs began rushing into the Indians' sacred Black Hills in search of gold, tensions escalated. The result was one of the most significant battles of the American West: Little Big Horn, also known as "Custer's Last Stand." In June 1876, Lieutenant Colonel George Custer and the 7th Cavalry were trapped and wiped out by a much larger Native-American force led by legendary warriors Sitting Bull and Crazy Horse. The Indians won that day, but reprisals were swift and harsh. The battle turned out to be the last stand of the Lakota Sioux and Cheyenne as well.

George Custer

# ANIMALS ON MONTANA'S PLAINS

IN MONTANA, CATTLE RANCHING is high-tech. The Northern Livestock Video Auction broadcasts its auctions by satellite from Billings. The wide-open plains where cattle now roam were once home to dinosaurs, and Montana seems to have been a favored stomping ground. In 2000, a paleontologist at Montana State University's Museum of the Rockies discovered a T-Rex specimen in the town of Jordan — one stop on the "Montana Dinosaur Trail." The discovery made history, in part because it yielded bone tissue common to female birds. That same year, a remarkably preserved, 22-foot-long, duck-billed dinosaur was also discovered. His mummified state enabled paleontologists to even identify the contents of his stomach.

# THE CORNHUSKER STATE

More than 93 percent of Nebraska's land is used for agriculture, and the state is a top-five producer of both corn and beef. In fact, cattle outnumber people here. You can also thank Nebraska for Kool-Aid®, invented here in 1927, as well as the Swanson® frozen TV dinner, invented in 1953.

At one time, the state's flat plains didn't have a lot of trees, so Nebraskans introduced Arbor Day to promote tree planting, giving a new ritual to school kids everywhere. They don't grow cars in Nebraska, so Carhenge is a little harder to explain. Built in 1987, Carhenge consists of 38 cars, painted gray, springing out of the ground in homage to England's famous Stonehenge. The site has become a minor tourist attraction for the town of Alliance, although not many druids show up.

*Greetings from Nebraska* — home of the nation's only unicameral (one-house) legislature.

GREETINGS from NEBRASKA

USA 37

2002

62

# SOD BUSTERS

BLACKSMITH JOHN DEERE first manufactured his cast steel plow in 1837 — breaking up the Midwest's tough soil and preparing the way for a giant opportunity. The Homestead Act of 1862 opened vast areas of government land to anyone willing to build a home on a parcel of land and live there for five years. Deere's invention busted a lot of sod; in many cases, a shortage of trees meant that sod was used as building material for the new homesteads.

Daniel Freeman was the country's first homesteader, outside the Nebraska town of Beatrice. He filed his claim 10 minutes after midnight on the day the Homestead Act took effect. Another notable Nebraska homesteader was Robert Ball Anderson, a freed slave and Civil War veteran. Over the years, he eventually amassed more than 2,000 acres of land.

# BUFFALO BILL

WILLIAM FREDERICK CODY won the nickname "Buffalo Bill" in an eight-hour hunting contest. For a time, he made his living hunting buffalo to feed construction crews for the Kansas Pacific Railroad. By Cody's count, he killed 4,280 buffalo in 17 months.

Within a few short years, the wild West was getting a lot less wild. In 1883, Cody debuted "Buffalo Bill's Wild West" in North Omaha, to celebrate a vanishing era. The show was wildly popular, touring for many years — including a royal performance for Queen Victoria. Each performance featured extravagant scenes from the American West using authentic characters, such as the Sioux chief, Sitting Bull. Often the show ended with a dramatic depiction of Custer's Last Stand, with Cody playing General Custer. William Cody died in 1917. Reports of his last words carried his characteristic theatrical flair: "Let my show go on."

Greetings from NEVADA

37 USA

2002

## ///////// THE SILVER STATE

This state is best known for what goes on in the desert valley that includes Las Vegas, yet Nevada has more mountain ranges than any other state. Speaking of Vegas, it's been the fastest-growing metropolitan area for years, growing 83 percent between 1990 and 2000. All those newcomers will have a place to crash if they've got the money, because Las Vegas has more hotel rooms than any other city in the world. Spending one night in each room would take centuries. But Nevada just doesn't have that kind of time. President Lincoln was in such a hurry to add Nevada to the union that the state's constitution was delivered to Washington, D.C., by telegraph via Morse code: all 16,543 words. *Greetings from Nevada* — the only state with a museum entirely devoted to Liberace.

# The COMSTOCK LODE

TODAY, NEVADA PRODUCES MORE GOLD than any other state and trails only South Africa and Australia in worldwide production. In fact, it was Nevada's gold that enticed miners to the state in the 1850s. Many grew frustrated by the tenacious mud — "blue stuff" that clung to their picks and boots. Little did those first miners know that blue mud signaled one of the largest silver deposits ever discovered.

Some say that Henry Tompkins Paige Comstock talked his way into an early claim by convincing two other miners that he owned the land. At any rate, he sold the claim for a fraction of its eventual worth. By 1878, the Comstock Lode had produced more than $400 million in silver ore — even though the vast majority of mining companies operating in the region at the time actually lost money. One of those who failed as a miner decided to give writing a try. So Samuel Clemens began writing for a Nevada newspaper, where he first used the pen name Mark Twain.

# AREA 51

IT'S HARD TO PIN DOWN the actual name for the military facility at Groom Lake. Official records are as scarce as water on the dry lake bed, but in the public imagination, the facility is known as "Area 51." That name comes from the grid square on maps of the massive Nevada Test Site — the region set aside long ago for nuclear testing.

Area 51's secrecy provides easy fodder for UFO conspiracy theorists. In 1996, Nevada's government acknowledged the public's fascination with the area by renaming a section of nearby Nevada State Route 375 as "The Extraterrestrial Highway." Oddly, no records of traffic citations given to UFOs are available.

Greetings From NEW HAMPSHIRE

USA 37

2002

//////////// **THE GRANITE STATE** New Hampshire marks history as both the first state to lose a native son in the Civil War and — almost exactly a century later — the first to send one of its own into space: Alan Shepard, in May 1961. The entire country mourned along with New Hampshire when it lost its teacher-astronaut, Christa McAuliffe, in the 1986 Challenger disaster.

Just beneath New Hampshire's hills lies the source of its nickname. Of all the granite here, one natural rock formation was a treasured symbol for nearly 200 years: the Old Man of the Mountain, which collapsed in 2003 but is preserved on the New Hampshire quarter. Speaking of mountains, Mt. Washington, the state's tallest precipice, holds the all-time surface wind-speed record not associated with a tornado or hurricane: 231 mph.

*Greetings from New Hampshire* — location of the nation's first women's labor strike, in 1828, at the Dover Cotton Factory.

# ★★★ NEW HAMPSHIRE
# PRIMARY

★ ★ ★ ★ ★ ★ ★ ★ ★

SINCE THE FIRST modern primary in 1952, New Hampshire has been considered a maker, and breaker, of presidential hopefuls. Generally considered to carry more weight than the Iowa caucuses, the primary is considered an early measurement of the national attitude toward the candidates for nomination. Incumbent Presidents Harry Truman and Lyndon Johnson dropped their re-election bids after poor showings in New Hampshire. In fact, only Bill Clinton and George W. Bush have won the presidency after losing this primary. The high stakes in New Hampshire attract reporters and candidates by the busload.

New Hampshire's small geographic size and relatively small population give presidential hopefuls the chance to visit the state frequently and engage in "retail politics." While voters in other states rely on 30-second TV spots to form opinions, New Hampshire voters make decisions based on personal contact at the general store.

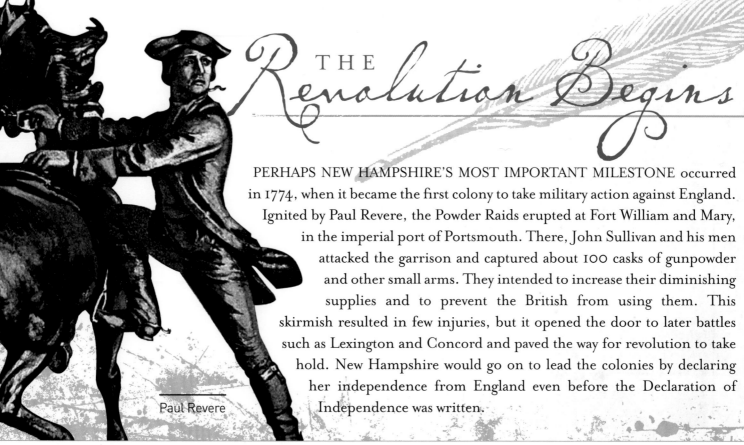

Paul Revere

## THE *Revolution Begins*

PERHAPS NEW HAMPSHIRE'S MOST IMPORTANT MILESTONE occurred in 1774, when it became the first colony to take military action against England. Ignited by Paul Revere, the Powder Raids erupted at Fort William and Mary, in the imperial port of Portsmouth. There, John Sullivan and his men attacked the garrison and captured about 100 casks of gunpowder and other small arms. They intended to increase their diminishing supplies and to prevent the British from using them. This skirmish resulted in few injuries, but it opened the door to later battles such as Lexington and Concord and paved the way for revolution to take hold. New Hampshire would go on to lead the colonies by declaring her independence from England even before the Declaration of Independence was written.

# THE GARDEN STATE

New Jersey's sense of heritage runs deep, largely due to the state's prominent role in the American Revolution. In the pre-dawn hours following Christmas night 1776, George Washington led his army across the icy waters of the Delaware River to launch a surprise attack on the British and their Hessian mercenaries. Washington's tactics led to a decisive early victory at the Battle of Trenton.

This little state is more than just a thoroughfare between New York and Philadelphia. On average, New Jerseyans earn almost 30 percent more each year than most Americans, and they lay claim to some of the wealthiest horse farms, with more horses per capita than any other state. New Jersey is also the most densely populated state, with about 1,000 people per square mile. *Greetings from New Jersey* — where you can choose from more than 600 diners for your next meal.

Greetings From NEW JERSEY

37 USA

2002

# Before TINSELTOWN

Thomas Edison (middle, seated) and company

MOVIEGOERS EVERYWHERE have New Jersey to thank for the ingenuity behind to-day's multibillion-dollar media industry. The electric light bulb and the Kinetascope (the earliest movie camera) were among more than a thousand patented inventions to come out of New Jersey — all courtesy of a certified genius named Thomas Edison.

By 1893, Edison had built the first movie studio — essentially a tarpaper shack next to his laboratories in West Orange. He brought in daylight through a skylight in the roof and put the entire studio on a turntable to maximize exposure to the sun. In 1903, Edison made what is now considered to be the first major narrative film, *The Great Train Robbery*. But before long, the movie industry moved to California, attracted in part by the year-round sunny weather and variety of shooting locations.

## BOARDWALK ATLANTIC CITY, NJ

IN 1852, the Camden & Atlantic Railroad made it possible for people to take a day trip from Philadelphia to Atlantic City. By the 1880s, Atlantic City was a flourishing tourist destination with grand hotels, elegant restaurants and a lively nightlife. Challenged to find a way to keep sand out of the hotels and rail cars, a railroad conductor named Alexander Boardman came up with the idea of a wooden promenade — and the boardwalk was born.

Atlantic City nightclubs have showcased some of the nation's great talents, many of whom launched their careers here in the 1930s to 1950s. Frank Sinatra, Jerry Lewis, and Abbott & Costello all have early ties to Atlantic City. By the late '60s, Atlantic City tourism was in a slump. Casino gambling was introduced in 1976, bringing with it a new wave of luxury hotels and high rises, which would once again put this seaside town in the spotlight.

GREETINGS FROM NEW MEXICO

USA 37

2002

AAA 398
AUGUST 6, 1945

//////////// THE LAND OF ENCHANTMENT New Mexico has more cattle than people, yet more Ph.D.s per capita than any other state in the nation. British entrepreneur Richard Branson is building a spaceport here for Virgin® Galactic, his passenger spaceflight enterprise. Of course, it might not be New Mexico's first connection to outer space. The state is famous for a 1947 incident when the Air Force issued a press release announcing the recovery of a crashed "flying disc," only to retract it the next day. In addition to skepticism surrounding UFOs, New Mexico is also home to countless myths surrounding the life of Billy the Kid. According to legend, he killed 21 men — likely more than twice the actual number.

*Greetings from New Mexico* — home of Acoma Pueblo, a fortress known as "Sky City," which current residents claim has been continuously inhabited since before the 10th century.

# LOS ALAMOS LABORATORIES

UNTIL 1943, LOS ALAMOS Ranch School was a private school for boys. Then it was bought by the federal government and became home to the most critical and secret effort of World War II: The Manhattan Project.

Within 27 months, a team of some of the world's most brilliant scientists had worked through extraordinary technical challenges to create three atomic devices. The first was tested in an area of the New Mexico desert known as *Jornada del Muerto* — "Journey of the Dead Man." The other two bombs were used on Hiroshima and Nagasaki.

In the years following the war, Los Alamos National Laboratory continued weapons research, but it also branched out into a wide variety of disciplines, including cosmology, alternative energy research, advanced computing and nanotechnology.

# Zozobra

HAD A BAD YEAR? Burn it. Every September, the people of Santa Fe observe *Fiestas de Santa Fe*, celebrating the day when Don Diego de Vargas recaptured their city from Pueblo Indians in 1692. In 1924, Santa Fe artist Will Shuster added a new twist: a giant wood-and-cloth marionette, stuffed with the shredded remnants of the previous year, such as bad report cards, copies of police reports, even divorce papers. The effigy is called *Zozobra*, based on the Spanish word for "anxiety."

At the end of the annual celebration, tens of thousands of participants chant, "Burn him!" as the giant figure — also known as "Old Man Gloom" — is set ablaze, sending a year's bad memories up in smoke.

## ///////// THE EMPIRE STATE

For many, New York means New York City, and why not? New York City was once the capital of the United States; George Washington was sworn in as president in Lower Manhattan. Dominant in finance, advertising, media and culture, New York City is like no other. Five of her skyscrapers could each, at one time, have claimed to be the "world's tallest building."

But New York State goes far beyond the five boroughs of New York City. The state was home to the oldest cattle ranch in America and the first brewery. It opened the first state park in America: Niagara Falls. And the massive Adirondack State Park is larger than Yellowstone, Yosemite, Grand Canyon, Glacier and Olympic Parks combined. *Greetings from New York* — the second-largest apple producer in the nation and home of the "Big Apple."

Empire State Building

# New Amsterdam

BEFORE THERE WAS NEW YORK, there was New Amsterdam — a Dutch trading settlement on the southern tip of Manhattan Island. Established in 1626, New Amsterdam was part of the broader New Netherlands colony. As the area grew prosperous, it captured the attention of England's King Charles II. The king dispatched his brother, the Duke of York, and granted him vast American territories, including areas held by the Dutch. When the Duke of York showed up with his fleet, the Dutch governor gave up without resistance — and New Amsterdam became New York.

The Dutch presence in New Amsterdam is still visible today. Their bustling trading center was located behind a giant wall, built to protect from Indian invasion. Today, that same line is called "Wall Street." Nearby Dutch villages of *Haarlem* and *Breukelen* evolved into today's Harlem and Brooklyn. The commercial vigor that made New Amsterdam a tempting target eventually transformed New York City into the financial capital of the world.

# THE Erie Canal

BEGUN IN 1817, the Erie Canal was an engineering marvel, but not everyone agreed at the time. Critics called it "Clinton's Ditch," for New York Governor DeWitt Clinton, a major advocate of the canal. And it was quite a ditch: 363 miles long and 4 feet deep, providing a continuous channel of water from New York Harbor to the Great Lakes. As a result, Rochester, Syracuse and Buffalo became industrial centers, opening markets to both New York City and the emerging West.

Completed in 1825, the canal was such an immediate success that it was expanded with a second canal, beginning just 10 years later. In 1903, a third canal was begun — the Barge Canal — which is still in use today.

# THE TAR HEEL STATE

Natural resources have long played a part in this state's history — from the tar that stuck to the heels of laborers and soldiers alike, to gold. In 1799, 12-year-old Conrad Reed pulled a shiny rock from a creek on his family's farm. His father used it as a doorstop. Three years later, they decided to have the 17-pound yellow rock examined — and North Carolina's gold rush was born, decades before California's. More recently, North Carolina has coaxed a different kind of gold from the ground: tobacco, still the state's No. 1 crop.

North Carolina was last to secede from the Union but lost 40,000 lives in the Civil War, more than any other Confederate state. The citizen-warrior tradition continues at Fort Bragg, one of the largest military installations in the world and home of the 82nd Airborne Division.

*Greetings from North Carolina* — where locals grapple with Ohio over the origins of aviation and with Florida over the origins of NASCAR®.

2002

74

# THE LOST Colony

IN AUGUST 1587, JOHN WHITE LEFT a fledgling colony at Roanoke Island and traveled to England for critically needed supplies. He hoped to return to North Carolina within a few months, but the Spanish Armada had other plans. Tensions between England and Spain blocked his return. By the time White was able to organize a return trip with properly outfitted vessels, three years had passed. When he finally arrived back at Roanoke Island, the place was deserted. There were no signs of violence, just a single word—"CROATOAN"—carved into a tree in the encampment.

White suspected the 117 colonists had fled for Croatoan Island to the south, but before he could stage a search, a hurricane forced his return to England. White died years later — never able to finance a trip to search for the lost colonists and leaving behind a mystery unsolved to this day.

# WOOLWORTH'S AND CIVIL RIGHTS

ON FEBRUARY 1, 1960, FOUR AFRICAN-AMERICAN college students sat down at the whites-only lunch counter at F. W. Woolworth's in Greensboro. They didn't get lunch that day, but they got attention — and that changed everything. After holding their seats until closing time, the four protesters returned with a few more the next day. By the end of the week, hundreds had shown up.

The sit-in at Greensboro inspired similar efforts throughout the South, and it eventually helped change segregation laws and the course of the Civil Rights Movement. Today, that 8-foot section of the lunch counter resides with Abe Lincoln's hat and Thomas Jefferson's Bible at the Smithsonian National Museum of American History.

Greetings from NORTH DAKOTA

USA 37

2002

MY VIEWS

## /////////// THE PEACE GARDEN STATE

Sibling rivalry can be tough between twins, so one has to wonder about the Dakotas. They became states on the same day, so no one really knows which was born first. The alphabet says that North Dakota was the 39th and South Dakota the 40th state. Even so, legislators have attempted three times to remove "North" from the state's name. All three attempts failed in the statehouse.

Despite the twin status, North Dakota stands out as most central: The town of Rugby is the exact geographic center of North America. This state is also central for safety, according to the FBI, whose statistics consistently identify North Dakota as the safest state in the nation. *Greetings from North Dakota* — whose nickname refers to the botanical garden that straddles the North Dakota/Manitoba international boundary.

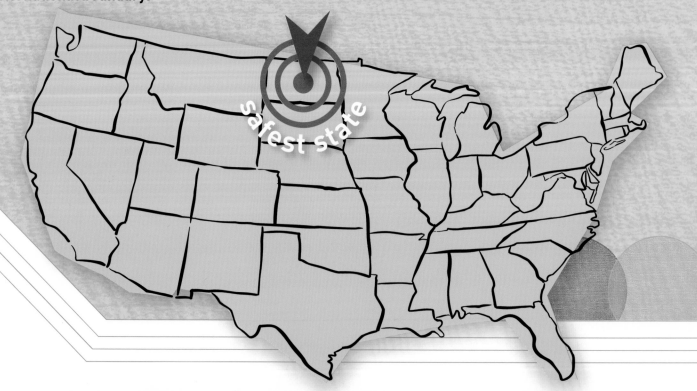

safest state

# Teddy Roosevelt

THEODORE "TEDDY" ROOSEVELT'S DIARY entry on February 14, 1884, was as brief as it was haunting: "The light has gone out of my life." Both his young wife and his mother died in the same house on that day. Somehow, he needed to start over.

Later that year, Roosevelt moved from New York to North Dakota, where he had first traveled on a hunting trip in 1883. Though he lived in the state less than three years, Roosevelt established two cattle ranches and deepened his love for the environment — which helped shape his conservation efforts as the 26th president of the United States. "I never would have been president if it had not been for my experiences in North Dakota," he said.

# Homesteaders

TODAY, THE WINDSWEPT PLAINS of North Dakota are generating a lot of buzz about generating a lot of energy. Wind energy may be the future, but in North Dakota's past, harsh winters required people of hardy stock to work the land. Enter the Scandinavians.

When the Dakota Territory was opened to homesteading in 1863, newcomers were offered 160 acres of land each. This brought a boom of immigration from Norway, Sweden and Germany. So strong were the immigration patterns that by 1915, roughly 80 percent of the state's population consisted of immigrants and the children of immigrants.

Over the years, homesteaders had more than their share of difficulties. Due to North Dakota's drier climate, it was not easy to support a family on a standard homestead plot. Many farms failed or consolidated, yet the cultural heritage of generations of immigrant farmers continues to this day.

Greetings from **OHIO**

37 USA

2002

//////////// **THE BUCKEYE STATE** Despite a down-home nickname tied to the state tree, Ohio seems to have a special relationship with people who reach for the sky. The Wright brothers first experimented with airplane design here, and it's the birthplace of both John Glenn and Neil Armstrong — the first American to orbit the Earth and the first person to set foot on the moon, respectively.

This state calls itself the Mother of Modern Presidents, yet the names of the seven Ohio-born presidents don't necessarily leap to mind: Grant, Hayes, Garfield, Harrison (Benjamin), McKinley, Taft and Harding. They are not the most lauded in history books, nor the luckiest: three of the seven died in office. Ohio has much better luck with its sports teams. *Greetings from Ohio* — host of the first professional baseball team, the Cincinnati Red Stockings.

# THE FLAMING CUYAHOGA RIVER

**W**ITH MAJOR CITIES located on the Cuyahoga River and its easy access to Lake Erie, Ohio quickly became a strategic place for manufacturing. Oil tycoon John D. Rockefeller opened his first refinery in Cleveland in 1863. Eight years later, Benjamin Goodrich established his rubber factory in Akron. Other heavy industries such as iron, steel and coal also thrived. This was long before today's extensive environmental regulation, so untold tons of toxic industrial waste ended up in Ohio's waterways.

By the 1960s, Lake Erie was virtually dead, and the Cuyahoga River was horribly polluted. In fact, it caught fire on several occasions. The blaze on June 22, 1969, finally captured the nation's attention, leading eventually to the Clean Water Act of 1972 and the creation of the U.S. Environmental Protection Agency.

## The Soap Box Derby

ONE OF OHIO'S MOST POPULAR recreational events produces no pollution at all: the annual All-American Soap Box Derby, drawing entrants from across the nation and around the world. It all began in Dayton in 1933, with cars made out of anything and everything. If you could add wheels, you could race it. The first officially organized race included 362 children. By 1936, the world had caught on and the race had its first official international entry — from South Africa. Using gravity alone, racers can reach speeds of up to 30 mph. The fast-moving race was slower to officially admit girls: not until 1971. Today, girls comprise almost half of all entrants.

# //////////// THE SOONER STATE

Although Oklahoma has more man-made lakes than any other state, underground is where you'll find the state's most famous liquid: oil. Tulsa was once called the "oil capital of the world," and there's even an oil well drilled to reach reserves beneath the State Capitol building.

The state made headlines around the world on April 19, 1995 — the day bombs claimed 168 lives as they destroyed the Murrah Federal Building in Oklahoma City. Until the 2001 attacks on the World Trade Center, Oklahoma's tragedy ranked as the deadliest act of terrorism on U.S. soil.

*Greetings from Oklahoma* — whose nickname originated in 1889, when President Benjamin Harrison opened up unassigned land to settlers and some tried to sneak in "sooner" than allowed.

Greetings from OKLAHOMA

2002

# INDIAN TERRITORY

OKLAHOMA HAS THE NATION'S SECOND-LARGEST POPULATION of Native Americans — nearly 400,000. Those numbers reflect the bitter history of our country's Indian relocation policies. In 1830, the U.S. government designated this region for resettlement in the Indian Removal Act. Many different tribes were forced west to Oklahoma, along the Trail of Tears. At one point they joined together in hopes of establishing an Indian state, but their efforts were not successful. The state's name is based on two words from the Choctaw language, meaning "red man." Some 37 different federally recognized tribes live in Oklahoma, and most do not live on reservations.

# THE DUST BOWL

LESS THAN 50 YEARS after the state's first great land rush, a combination of prolonged drought plus misuse of land turned the rich farmland into a wasteland. Oklahoma had become part of the Dust Bowl. The resulting agricultural devastation lengthened the Depression for already hard-hit Oklahoma farmers. Some estimate that as much as one-quarter of the state's inhabitants fled west. Many ended up in California, where they were not welcome. In fact, the Los Angeles Police Department set up border patrols, to try to keep them out. Roadside camps began filling with migrant workers, inspiring John Steinbeck's *The Grapes of Wrath*. In 1933, Franklin D. Roosevelt was elected president and introduced the New Deal, his program of poverty relief and reform. By 1941, the drought had relented — on the eve of another national crisis, World War II.

Greetings from OREGON

USA 37

2002

## /////////// THE BEAVER STATE

With its tall, dense forests in the western part of the state, Oregon was historically one of the nation's leaders in timber production. Yet controversy between environmentalists and the timber industry led to change. During the 1990s, public interest in protecting wildlife habitat increased, while timber production declined. Oregon *does* lead the nation in growing such delicacies as peppermint, blackberries and boysenberries.

This state's great outdoors also contains several active volcanoes. Thousands of years ago, one of Oregon's volcanoes collapsed; in its center lies Crater Lake, the deepest lake in the country and seventh-deepest in the world. *Greetings from Oregon* — where a graphic-design student at Portland State University designed the famous Nike® "swoosh" in 1971.

# FUJITA'S SURPRISE

AFTER PEARL HARBOR, every state was on high alert for another attack. Yet Oregon was the only place in the lower 48 states to actually be bombed by manned Japanese aircraft. On September 9, 1942, a Japanese submarine surfaced off Oregon's coast, and two officers in the Japanese Imperial Navy climbed into a seaplane mounted on the sub's deck. Their mission was to drop incendiary bombs on some of Oregon's wilderness in an attempt to start fast-spreading fires that would lead to the destruction of towns and cause overall panic. However, the attack did limited damage. A subsequent attack, on September 29, started no fires.

The pilot's name was Nobuo Fujita. He survived the war, became a prosperous businessman, and in 1962 returned to Oregon in a gesture of peace between Japan and the United States.

# The OREGON TRAIL

IN 1805, THE STATE'S WATERWAYS brought explorers Lewis and Clark to coastal Oregon. Their journey marked the end of the Oregon Trail, which started in Independence, Missouri, and stretched for about 2,000 miles westward. Native Americans and trappers had forged parts of the trail earlier, but Lewis and Clark's expedition made it famous.

Thousands of settlers soon began following the trail in one of the nation's great migrations — some seeking rich farmland, others yearning for California gold. The most famous tragedy on the trail was that of the Donner party, in winter 1846-47. Unable to cross the Sierra Nevada Mountains before winter set in, 41 died out of their group of 87. Some of the others resorted to eating human flesh in order to survive. The last of the survivors finally reached their destination a full year after they had started. The great trek west on the Oregon Trail finally dwindled in 1869, with the completion of the Transcontinental Railroad.

Greetings from PENNSYLVANIA

37 USA

2002

## THE KEYSTONE STATE

This state held a position in the center — the keystone, as it were — of the original 13 colonies. Philadelphia also served as the first U.S. capital. It was here, in Independence Hall, that the Founding Fathers finalized the pivotal documents of our democracy: the Declaration of Independence, the Articles of Confederation and the U.S. Constitution.

But Pennsylvania has not remained in the past. Indeed, it was the first state to put its Web address on its license plates. While many know of the state's resident chocolatier, Hershey®, fewer know that the state is also the birthplace of ketchup, created in 1876 by Henry J. Heinz. (A food shortage during and after World War II kept the product off shelves for almost a decade). *Greetings from Pennsylvania* — home of Punxsutawney Phil, the weather-forecasting groundhog.

84

# The Centralia Fire

THERE'S A TOWN IN CENTRAL PENNSYLVANIA THAT HAS BEEN ON FIRE, literally, for more than 40 years. The Centralia mine fire started in 1962, when residents set fire to a trash pit and inadvertently ignited a concealed vein of coal. The fire eventually spread through a network of abandoned mines beneath the city, and every attempt to extinguish it failed. By the late '60s, residents began leaving their homes, due to deadly gases.

On Valentine's Day 1981, a patch of ground collapsed beneath the feet of a 12-year-old boy, who was barely rescued. Beneath him, the deep hole leaked lethal amounts of carbon monoxide. The accident made national news, and Congress appropriated $42 million to begin buying out and relocating property owners.

From a population of more than 1,000 in the 1980s, Centralia now houses fewer than 20. Streets are eerily silent, while smoke continues to billow from cracks in the earth. It's estimated that the fire could continue burning for another 100 years or more.

# THE Steel State

ON THE OUTSKIRTS OF PITTSBURGH, Scottish immigrant Andrew Carnegie began building his steel empire with his first order, in 1875, for 2,000 steel rails. Efficiency was a mantra for Carnegie, who began purchasing everything needed to make his steel—from the fields containing the raw deposits to the railroads that transported them. The demand for steel continued to grow throughout the first half of the 20th century.

By the late 1960s, however, the U.S. steel industry began to decline, due in part to labor troubles and an unwillingness to innovate. Mills closed, jobs disappeared and Pittsburgh joined other post-industrial areas now known as the Rust Belt. Today, some of the mines that once supplied crucial limestone for the steel process are used for growing mushrooms or storing archival materials.

# THE OCEAN STATE

If you live here, chances are you regard "small" as particularly valuable. Such is the case with license-plate numbers, for example. Here, smaller numbers mean greater status; some small-numbered plates have been kept in Rhode Island families for generations. The state is small in size too: 48 miles long by 37 miles wide. Yet it has the longest official name in the nation: "State of Rhode Island and Providence Plantations."

In other claims to fame, Rhode Island is one of only two states that never ratified the 18th Amendment, although it was neighboring Maine that put the first Prohibition law into motion.

The Industrial Revolution also started here in 1790 when Samuel Slater constructed a water-powered, cotton-spinning mill in Pawtucket. *Greetings from Rhode Island* — whose name comes from a Dutch explorer and means "red island," due to the red clay.

*Greetings from* **RHODE ISLAND** USA**37**

2002

The Breakers

# Millionaires' PLAYGROUND

THE GILDED AGE of the late 1800s came to full flower in Newport, where the moneyed elite built fabulous mansions known as "summer cottages." The town's high society was created by the grand dame of the Gilded Age, Caroline Webster Schermerhorn Astor — known simply as Mrs. Astor. The Astor summer home, Beechwood, became the center of the social season, and Mrs. Astor did not look favorably upon those with "new money," such as the Vanderbilts.

The Vanderbilts built two mansions in Newport: Marble House and The Breakers. Marble House stands next door to Beechwood and was an $11 million birthday gift to Alva Vanderbilt in 1892.

The early 1920s witnessed Newport's last golden summers. Soon after, taxes eroded the vast fortunes and the Great Depression began. Many mansions were demolished — some after fire damage, others for subdivisions. A number were turned into museums and a few remain in private hands.

# Roots of Tolerance

Roger Williams

IN 1630, PURITANS began arriving in the New World, eager to find the religious freedom denied them by the Church of England. Soon, however, some of those same Puritans began pressuring other colonists to worship as they did. One minister in Salem, Massachusetts, spoke out against the hypocrisy. Roger Williams advocated religious tolerance, using language later echoed by Thomas Jefferson in a bill that would lead to our country's First Amendment in 1786. Eventually, Williams was thrown out of the Massachusetts Bay Colony. In 1636, he traveled to what is now Rhode Island and established the settlement of Providence. Soon, others seeking the same freedoms joined him. He later obtained a royal charter from King Charles II, granting the colony full liberty of conscience.

Greetings from SOUTH CAROLINA

37 USA

2002

## //////////// THE PALMETTO STATE

South Carolina never had a problem being first. Three months before the Declaration of Independence, the state declared itself sovereign from Britain. In 1860, it was the first Southern state to secede from the Union. In fact, the first shots of the Civil War were fired in South Carolina, at Fort Sumter, although no blood was shed there.

South Carolina was also home to generations of pioneering African-American performers, including singers James Brown, Chubby Checker and Dizzy Gillespie. Lesser known is Clayton "Peg Leg" Bates, a tap dancer who made 21 appearances on the "The Ed Sullivan Show," despite an amputated left leg. *Greetings from South Carolina* — where, in 1954, Strom Thurmond became the first person elected to the U. S. Senate by write-in vote.

CIVIL WAR CENTENNIAL
FORT SUMTER
1861 1961
4¢
UNITED STATES POSTAGE

Fort Sumter

# Gullah ('gələ)

THE ISLANDS OFF the southern coast of South Carolina were isolated for years — accessible only by water until the 1950s. But that isolation provided a shelter for a language and culture that could easily have been lost. Also known as Sea Island Creole, the language of Gullah is spoken by people along the coast of South Carolina and Georgia. The language was created by slaves and is a blend of English and various indigenous West African languages. It is believed that the word *Gullah* was derived from *Angola*, the original home of many slaves who arrived on the island's shores.

Efforts to preserve the language have born fruit, with a Gullah translation of the New Testament published in 2005 — 26 years in the making.

# The Hunley

ON FEBRUARY 17, 1864, the Confederate *H.L. Hunley* set naval history with the first successful submarine attack. Unfortunately, the crew of the *Hunley* fared no better than its target.

The *Hunley* — nearly 40 feet long with a crew of eight — slipped into Charleston Harbor during a severe Union blockade. Its torpedo was a bomb attached to a ramming spar. The submarine was spotted, but too late. An explosion sank the Union Navy's largest war ship, the *USS Housatonic*. Moments later, the *Hunley* surfaced to signal victory, then disappeared beneath the water.

The *Hunley* lay in the silt outside of Charleston Harbor for 131 years. Discovered in 1995, it was brought to the surface five years later. Inside were the skeletal remains of all eight crew members, who were buried in 2004 with full military honors.

Greetings *from* **SOUTH DAKOTA**

USA **37**

2002

## THE MOUNT RUSHMORE STATE

If you need some space, come to South Dakota. With an estimated 10 people per square mile, there's plenty of room — unless you're in Sturgis, whose population swells to nearly half a million every August, when thousands of motorcycles come roaring in. Starting with just nine riders in 1938, the Sturgis Motorcycle Rally is now considered the world's largest and brings in millions of dollars.

If it's corn you're after, head over to Mitchell for the Corn Palace Festival, where festivities center on an exhibition hall decorated entirely with grain. A local tradition since 1892, the murals on the exterior of Mitchell Corn Palace are redesigned each spring using thousands of bushels of native South Dakota corn, grain and grasses. At the end of the festival, it all goes to the birds. *Greetings from South Dakota* — home to Harney Peak, America's highest point east of the Rockies.

# The Badlands

Bighorn sheep

THE SIOUX NAMED this place *mako sica* (literally, "bad land") because it was such difficult terrain for travelers. For today's naturalist, however, a trip to the Badlands National Park is anything but bad. It contains nearly 244,000 acres of buttes, pinnacles, spires, ravines and gulches amid the country's largest protected mixed-grass prairie — at last count, 56 different kinds of grasses.

Native Americans were aware of the area's abundance and made use of it as a prime hunting ground for thousands of years. Some of the world's richest Oligocene fossil beds also exist here, drawing paleontologists from all corners of the globe for exploration into the origins of such animals as horses and dogs.

Not all animals of the Badlands are fossilized. Bighorn sheep, bison and the prairie rattler all make their home here. And if you're lucky, you might catch a glimpse of the black-footed ferret — one of America's most endangered mammals.

# MOUNTAIN MONUMENTS

CONSIDERED ONE OF AMERICA'S enduring monuments to democracy, Mt. Rushmore towers over the Black Hills at more than 5,500 feet above sea level. The monument depicts the faces of George Washington, Thomas Jefferson, Theodore Roosevelt and Abraham Lincoln. American-born sculptor Gutzon Borglum began work on the monument in 1927 at age 60 and worked with nearly 400 men, until his death in 1941. The monument was actually never finished, as Borglum's original plans called for inclusion of each president's torso down to the waist.

Ongoing controversy surrounding Native American land-ownership rights in the Black Hills led to the creation of another monument nearby. Begun in 1948 to honor the great Oglala chief, Crazy Horse, the sculpture remains a work in progress. Some predict that, when finished, it will be the largest in the world.

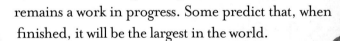

Mt. Rushmore

# THE VOLUNTEER STATE

Bordering eight states, Tennessee is within a day's drive of 75 percent of the U.S. population. Within its long borders lies the Great Smoky Mountains National Park — the nation's most-visited park — as well as Graceland, the final home and resting place of Elvis Presley. In addition to "The King," Tennessee produced three presidents: Andrew Jackson, James Polk and Andrew Johnson. Johnson worked his way through just about every political venue from city hall to the White House — rare in his time as well as now.

*Greetings from Tennessee — where the Grand Ole Opry® is the nation's longest-running radio broadcast, heard every Saturday night since 1925.*

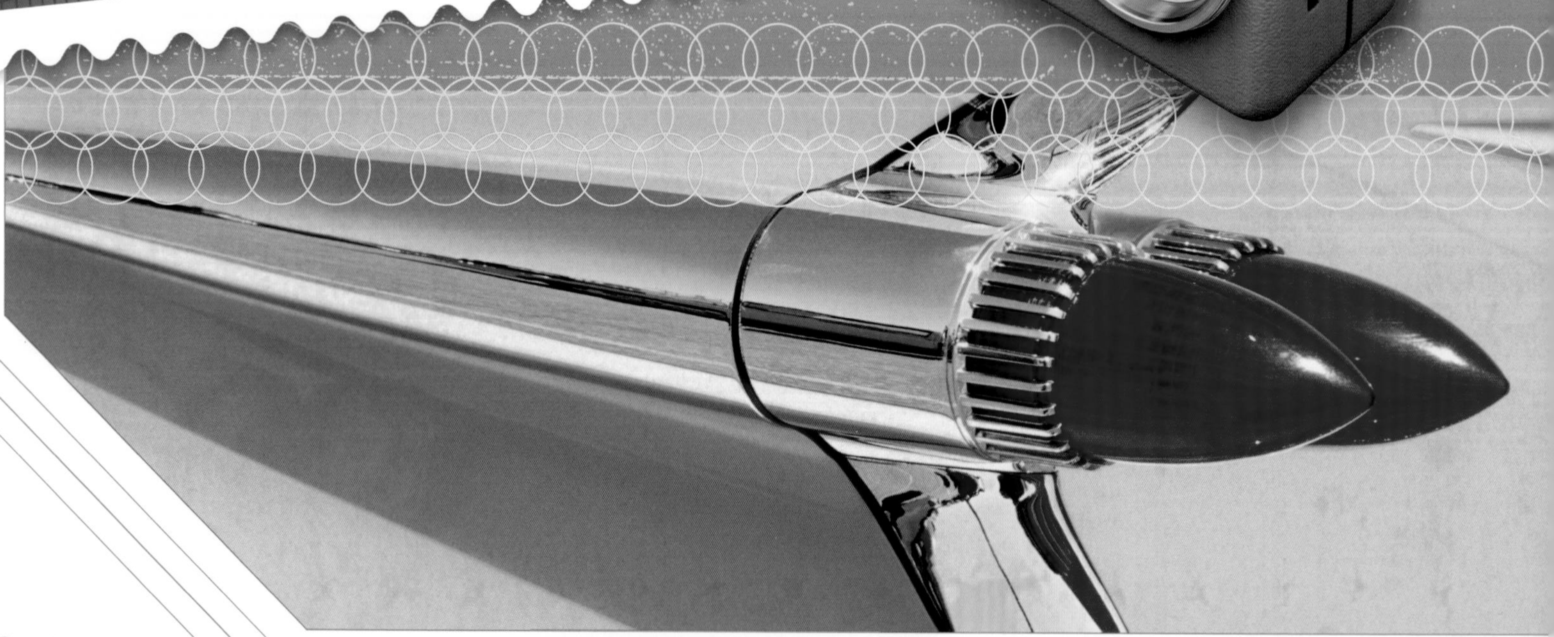

*Greetings from* TENNESSEE

**37** USA

2002

# DAVY CROCKETT

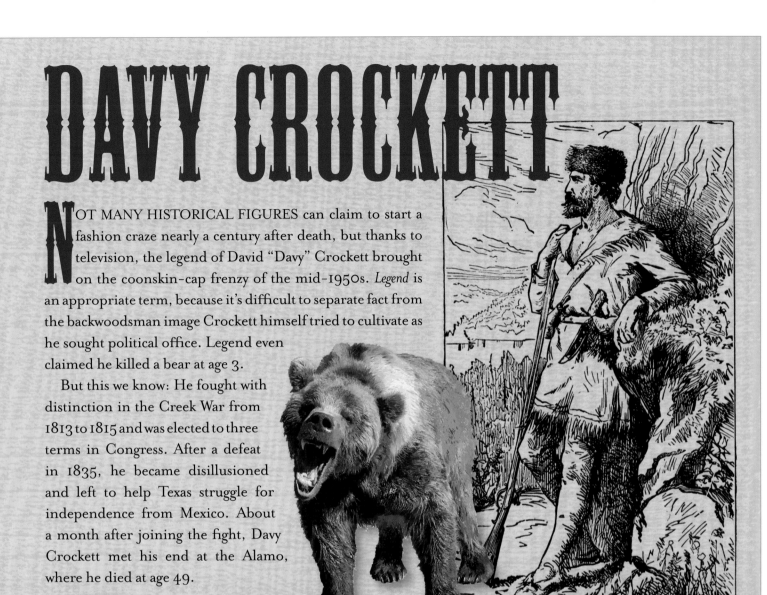

**N**OT MANY HISTORICAL FIGURES can claim to start a fashion craze nearly a century after death, but thanks to television, the legend of David "Davy" Crockett brought on the coonskin-cap frenzy of the mid-1950s. *Legend* is an appropriate term, because it's difficult to separate fact from the backwoodsman image Crockett himself tried to cultivate as he sought political office. Legend even claimed he killed a bear at age 3.

But this we know: He fought with distinction in the Creek War from 1813 to 1815 and was elected to three terms in Congress. After a defeat in 1835, he became disillusioned and left to help Texas struggle for independence from Mexico. About a month after joining the fight, Davy Crockett met his end at the Alamo, where he died at age 49.

Davy Crockett

# FROM 1812 TO THE GRIDIRON

TODAY, TENNESSEE VOLUNTEERS are celebrated on the courts and fields of athletic competition. But they earned their nickname on the fields of battle.

During the War of 1812, without asking for federal assistance, Tennessee's governor issued a call for 3,500 volunteers after an attack on Fort Mims, Alabama. Thousands responded. Later in the war, Tennessee's role in the Battle of New Orleans was decisive; the battle claimed more than 2,000 British casualties with fewer than 100 American losses.

Decades later, a nationwide call for 2,600 soldiers to volunteer from each state for the Mexican-American War was met by more than 30,000 Tennesseans. So strong was this tradition that, in 1905, "Tennessee Volunteers" became the official name for sports teams from the University of Tennessee.

# /////////// THE LONE STAR STATE

This state has experienced a tumultuous, cross-cultural history. After beginning as a Spanish colony, Texas next became a Mexican state, then a sovereign nation and, finally, a member of the United States.

When Texas joined the union in 1845, some believed it would be divided into more than one state, because it was so large. Indeed, it was the largest state until 1959, when Alaska joined the party. It's no surprise that Texas culture has a Spanish flavor. Between 1990 and 2004, the state's Latino population increased by almost 80 percent, and it's still growing. In several Texas cities, the Latino population is the majority.

*Greetings from Texas* — the state that loves its barbecue, its Friday-night high-school football and its larger-than-life reputation.

# SPINDLETOP OIL FIELD

AT THE TURN OF THE CENTURY, successful oil wells individually produced about 100 barrels of oil a day. That is, until January 1901, when a new Texas well near Beaumont spewed oil at least 150 feet into the air. It damaged the derrick and dumped almost 800,000 barrels into the surrounding fields before being capped nine days later. The gusher, drilled into the Spindletop Hill salt dome, marked the greatest oil discovery in U.S. history. Beaumont's population soon exploded, and more wells were drilled. The availability of petroleum products paved the way for an expanding automobile market. At one point, oil was so plentiful that it sold for only pennies a barrel.

# Remember the Alamo

IN THE EARLY 1820s, when Texas was a Mexican state, Mexico invited Americans to settle in its empty plains. A decade later, many of those same settlers turned against their hosts and fought for independence. The showdown of the Texas Revolution came in 1836, at the Alamo Mission. Defending the Alamo were Texians, a group of both Anglos and ethnic Mexicans. Opposing them was Mexican Gen. Antonio López de Santa Anna and his forces.

For 13 days the Texians fought off Santa Anna's troops, but they were outnumbered 10-to-1. Every defender was killed in the battle — or slaughtered afterward — including frontiersman Davy Crocket. The only survivors were a few women, children and slaves. The next month, Gen. Sam Houston exacted revenge for Texas at the Battle of San Jacinto, as his militiamen cried, "Remember the Alamo!" The swift victory — the fighting lasted less than 20 minutes — opened the door for the Republic of Texas to secede from Mexico, then join the United States in 1845. Still, it's the battle for the Alamo that's most remembered for the sacrifices made in the name of independence.

**37**ᵁˢᴬ

Greetings from

# UTAH

2002

THE BEEHIVE STATE

Once dismissed as a wasteland, this state is now regarded as a natural wonderland. Utah plays home to five national parks, seven national monuments, two national recreation areas and six national forests. Though snow is, by nature, wet, Utah's snow is celebrated for its dryness, which makes it lighter and great for skiing. Utah is also a magnet for anglers, but don't bother dropping a line into the state's biggest body of water. The Great Salt Lake is well-named — so salty that no fish live in it.

*Greetings from Utah* — a state whose nickname reflects its historical virtues of hard work and diligence, and where a golden spike symbolized completion of the Transcontinental Railroad in 1869 at Promontory Summit.

# The Promised Land

RELIGIOUS PERSECUTION PLAYED a key role in founding the nation and, at times, expanding it. After Joseph Smith was murdered by a mob in Illinois in 1844, the Mormon church's new leader, Brigham Young, declared the need for an exodus. The westward movement took Mormon pioneers out of this country into what was — when the migration began — a part of Mexico. Over the course of 23 years, about 70,000 Mormons migrated westward.

Although they originally left the United States to seek freedom, Mormon pioneers soon found themselves on American soil again, when the land they inhabited was acquired by the United States as part of the Utah Territory. But it would take decades to achieve statehood (as opposed to only four years, for neighboring Nevada). Politicians back East were apprehensive about the strength of the church's influence. After decades of failed attempts — and structural changes to ensure against theocracy — the seventh effort finally succeeded, in 1896.

Salt Lake Temple

# BONNEVILLE SALT FLATS

THE BONNEVILLE SALT FLATS WERE FORMED from the dry remains of a primordial lake that would rival Lake Michigan in size. They encompass an area so vast and smooth that, from certain angles, the curvature of the earth can be seen with the naked eye. For decades, the flats have been celebrated as nature's ultimate racetrack, the place to go for going fast. Of the 21 world land-speed records set since 1935, 18 were accomplished at Bonneville. The most recent record set there, which stood for 13 years, was by a jet-powered car driven by Gary Gabelich at 630 mph in 1970.

# THE GREEN MOUNTAIN STATE

Vermont's name comes from the French words *vert* and *mont*, meaning "green mountain." But when many tourists consider Vermont, they think not of green, but of red, orange and yellow — the changing colors of fall. Indeed, the state is heavily dependent upon tourism. Today's winter athletes owe their love of snowboarding to this state, where the first snowboard factory opened in 1977. The first ski resort to allow the sport was Vermont's own Suicide Six, in the town of Pomfret.

Vermont also stands out as the birthplace of the country's first patent recipient, and home of the first state constitution to outlaw slavery.

*Greetings from Vermont* — the nation's leading producer of maple syrup, more than 400,000 gallons a year.

*Greetings from* **VERMONT**

USA **37**

2002

## CONFEDERATES ATTACK Vermont

OVER THE COURSE OF THE CIVIL WAR, more than 30,000 Vermonters volunteered to serve with the Union Army. But on October 19, 1864, while many were away fighting, Confederates crossed into Vermont from, of all places, Canada. Led by Lieutenant Bennett Young, they attacked the small village of St. Albans, located on Lake Champlain, some 15 miles below the Canadian border. The Confederates rounded up residents at gunpoint and robbed several banks before retreating to Canada, where they were arrested and forced to return the money — although none were extradited.

DESPITE VERMONT'S BRUSH with the Civil War, people today are more likely to associate this state with ice cream — perhaps Cherry Garcia®, Karamel Sutra® or Phish Food®. Ben Cohen and Jerry Greenfield started their company here in 1978 after taking a $5 correspondence course in ice-cream making.

Early experimentations with flavors and textures brought delicious success: Within 10 years, Ben & Jerry's® had opened more than 80 shops in 18 states, and now it has close to 600 shops worldwide.

The company is also known for its commitment to social and environmental concerns. In 1985, it established The Ben & Jerry's Foundation, with a mission "to make the world a better place."

A scoop of Chunky Monkey®, anyone?

Greetings from *Virginia*

USA 37

2002

## THE OLD DOMINION

///////// If Virginia were a parent, it would probably have one of those bumper stickers about honors students. Virginia's sons were an over-achieving lot: Eight presidents to date (seven of the first 12) were born here. What's more, Virginia gave birth to other states. Portions of Michigan, Wisconsin, Minnesota, Indiana, Illinois and Ohio — and all of Kentucky and West Virginia — were once part of, or claimed by, the Virginia colony.

While steeped in history, Virginia is also widely celebrated for its beauty. In fact, although native-son Thomas Jefferson has long been admired for his writing, he published only a single full-length book. It was about — you guessed it — Virginia, in which he wrote extensively about the state and its natural wonders.

*Greetings from Virginia* — not a state, but a commonwealth, along with Kentucky, Massachusetts and Pennsylvania.

Thomas Jefferson

# THE PENTAGON

WITH ENTRY INTO WORLD WAR II looming, America's military faced a logistical crisis at home: 24,000 employees in 17 buildings spread across Washington, D.C. On a Thursday evening, Gen. Brehon Sommervell pulled together a team of engineers and architects and told them he needed plans for a new building — by Monday. The plans were as clever as they were quick: a five-sided building, composed of five concentric rings, five stories tall. The result was an incredibly efficient design. Although the Pentagon was, for years, the largest office building in the world, any point in the building can be reached within a seven-minute walk.

The Pentagon was built in just 16 months, with construction beginning on September 11, 1941 — 60 years to the day before a terrorist attack attempted to destroy this icon of American military power.

# BACON'S Rebellion

AS THE FIRST ENGLISH SETTLEMENT at Jamestown expanded inland in the 1670s, skirmishes with Native Americans grew more common and farmers began requesting greater protection. Gov. William Berkeley refused his cousin, Nathaniel Bacon, permission to raise a militia and lead expeditions against the Native Americans. Yet even without Berkeley's support, Bacon launched several raids.

When he returned to Jamestown, tensions grew worse between the two. After Berkeley granted and then revoked several concessions, Bacon and his men took over Jamestown. Bacon set up a new government and, during a siege that followed, had Jamestown burned to the ground.

About a month later, Bacon died suddenly of dysentery, and the rebellion was over. Berkeley responded by having 23 of Bacon's men put to death, a move so harsh that Berkeley was recalled to England and replaced as governor. But perhaps this first American revolt set the stage for a larger revolution a century later.

Nathaniel Bacon

## THE EVERGREEN STATE

Outsiders' perceptions about the rain in this state aren't truly accurate. Yes, it rains frequently here, but never very much at a time. In Seattle, an average year brings about 37 inches — less than New York City and far less than Miami. Perhaps the lack of sun adds to the perception; Seattle residents see more than 200 cloudy days per year. But if there's one thing that goes wonderfully well with this weather, it's hot coffee. And Seattle is home to both Starbucks® and Seattle's Best Coffee®.

The state's highest peak, Mount Rainier, is an active volcano that's part of the Ring of Fire. This ring of volcanic ranges stretches around the Pacific Ocean. *Greetings from Washington* — home to 500-some houseboats that dot the state's lakes and bays.

# GOLD BY THE TON

ALTHOUGH WASHINGTON NEVER HAD ITS OWN GOLD RUSH, the state's economy rose along with large discoveries elsewhere — especially the 1848 California Gold Rush and the later Klondike/Alaska strikes.

In July 1897, news raced through Seattle that "a ton of gold" was about to arrive at Schwabacher Wharf. Sure enough, the 68 miners on board the *S.S. Portland* had just returned from the Klondike River, in Canada's western Yukon Territory. The actual amount unloaded turned out to be 2 tons. Some say that before noon that day, passage on the *Portland* was fully booked for the return trip. Even the mayor, who was then attending a conference out of town, sent his resignation by telegraph and headed north.

Those who stayed behind took advantage of the opportunity to outfit and supply the excited, would-be miners who used Seattle as a launching point in their pursuit of gold. Other local industries flourished as well, including shipbuilding and lumber production.

# MOUNT *St. Helens*

ON MAY 18, 1980, AFTER about two months of steam eruptions and multiple earthquakes, Mount St. Helens exploded in a massive eruption that lasted for nine hours. The plume of ash extended at least 12 miles above sea level, and large amounts traveled eastward as far as Montana. Meanwhile, a giant debris landslide enveloped nearby towns, killing 57 people and countless animals, as well as destroying buildings, railroads and highways.

Although the volcano had been largely dormant since 1857, Native Americans who had lived nearby knew it was anything but silent — naming it *Louwala-Clough*, which means "smoking mountain."

Beyond the destruction, Mount St. Helens proved to be a valuable source of scientific information for geologists and volcanologists worldwide. In August 1982, President Ronald Reagan signed into law a measure establishing the Mount St. Helens National Volcanic Monument.

# THE MOUNTAIN STATE

Four states share a North/South distinction, but no other state is named "West" anything. Ingenious West Virginians have used their most-abundant natural resource as a building material, making houses entirely out of anthracite coal. One native son even captured a Guinness World Record™. On January 26, 1960, coaches and teammates decided that Danny Heater needed a basketball scholarship, so they kept feeding him the ball that night. Heater responded with 135 points, earning him a world record for points by one player in a single game — but not a scholarship.

*Greetings from West Virginia* — where if you tell someone to jump off a bridge, they just might. On Bridge Day every October, hundreds of people parachute and bungee jump off the New River Gorge Bridge.

Greetings from WEST VIRGINIA

USA 37

2002

New River Gorge Bridge

# Virginia Divided

THE CIVIL WAR PRODUCED a great number of tragedies and a great deal of history, but it also produced a new state.

When Virginia voted to secede from the Union, its western counties wanted to form a state of their own, but they faced a roadblock: The Constitution clearly stated that a new state could only break off from an existing one with permission from the original state. But Virginia had left the Union. The impasse was broken with a legislative sleight of hand. Western Virginia leaders organized a "restored" government for the state of Virginia. This new government, quickly recognized by Washington, then moved to formally grant *itself* permission to become the state of West Virginia.

After the war, Virginia repealed the permission and sued to have the western counties returned. In 1871, the U.S. Supreme Court sided with West Virginia, securing its position as the 35th state.

## Battle of BLAIR MOUNTAIN

THE RICH COAL FIELDS of West Virginia created the backdrop for perhaps the largest insurrection since the Civil War. In 1921, coal miners in the southwestern part of the state were struggling to join a union despite strong opposition from management. Tension turned to violence in late August, after the unpunished murder of a local police chief known for his pro-union sympathies. As many as 10,000 miners gathered along the Kanawha River, seeking to avenge the police chief's death. After 10 days and the loss of about 20 lives, federal troops were sent in to restore order, and the miners abandoned their battle.

Charges against the miners resulted in few convictions, but the event cost the labor cause dearly. Legal costs drained their coffers as membership throughout the union movement plummeted for years to come.

2002

## ///////////// THE BADGER STATE

In 1854, the Republican Party was born in this state out of a desire for a new political party that would oppose the spread of slavery into the western territories. The Harley-Davidson® motorcycle also got its start here, invented by two childhood friends in 1903: William S. Harley and Arthur Davidson.

When it comes to recreation, Wisconsinites love their Green Bay Packers® — the only nonprofit, community-owned team in the NFL™. Wherever you have football, you have tailgating, which leads to bratwurst and mustard. This state is home to the Mustard Museum, with varieties from 60 different countries.

But don't forget the cheese. More than 25 percent of the world's cheese is produced in the United States. And more than 25 percent of *that* (a whopping 2 billion-plus pounds a year) is produced here. *Greetings from Wisconsin* — nicknamed for early lead miners in the 1820s, who dug out holes in the hills, like badgers, in the cold winters.

106

# Wisconsin Shipwrecks

IN WISCONSIN'S EARLY YEARS, its link to the Atlantic Ocean was its connection with the Great Lakes. Don't be mislead by the benign term *lake*. More than 30 lighthouses stand guard on Wisconsin's shores, to guide sailors through what can amount to hurricane-force winds and 30-foot waves on Lake Superior and Lake Michigan.

The strength of those storms means that the Great Lakes are littered with sunken ships — remarkably preserved in the cold, fresh water. In November 1912, the schooner *Rouse Simmons* went down in a fierce gale, along with its entire crew and a cargo of freshly cut Christmas trees. Almost 60 years later, divers discovered the ship resting at the bottom of Lake Michigan. More than 700 such wrecks lie in Wisconsin's territorial waters.

# Milwaukee Breweries

AN INFLUX OF GERMAN immigrants in the 19th century brought not only the German culture but also the German beverage. At one point, nearly every community in the state had a brewery of its own. Eventually, those early brewers became household names. But in the late 1860s, each of them — Valentin Blatz, Frederick Miller, Joseph Schlitz and Frederick Pabst — was struggling to get a foothold in the national market.

Schlitz® gained market share when it shipped beer to Chicago after the devastating 1871 fire there, earning the slogan, "The Beer That Made Milwaukee Famous." In turn, Pabst® got its big break in 1893, at the Columbian Exposition in Chicago, when it beat out Anheuser-Busch® of St. Louis for the coveted blue ribbon. By the turn of the 20th century, Milwaukee had gained a reputation as America's leading city for beer and eventually earned the unofficial nickname "Brew City."

Greetings FROM WYOMING

USA **37**

2002

## //////// THE EQUALITY STATE

Wyoming was the first state to incorporate a symbol onto its license plates — appropriately, a cowboy. A fiercely independent frontier spirit characterizes this state, the one with the fewest people within its borders. In fact, Wyoming's independence almost prevented it from joining the union.

By the time Wyoming applied for statehood, in 1888, it had already allowed women to vote for 18 years. But congressional leaders threatened to withhold statehood unless women's suffrage in Wyoming was revoked. Leaders in Cheyenne sent back a tersely worded reply — stating, in effect, "We'd rather wait 100 years than join without women's suffrage." Within two years, Wyoming was welcomed to statehood, women voters and all. No wonder Wyoming is known as the "Equality State."

*Greetings from Wyoming* — where, in the 1930s, taxidermists Douglas and Ralph Herrick turned a practical joke into classic American folklore with their "jackalope."

Jackalope

"OLD FAITHFUL"

# YELLOWSTONE

A VETERAN OF LEWIS AND CLARK'S expeditions, John Colter decided to leave the group and become a fur trapper during the return leg of the second journey. Eventually, he became the first person of European descent to lay eyes on what would become Yellowstone National Park. When he returned East in 1810, his stories of hot springs, bubbling mudpots and exploding geysers were dismissed as delirium from wounds suffered during his explorations.

Ensuing decades brought back other explorers with similar tales, similarly dismissed. Expeditions between 1869 and 1871 finally documented that the claims were true. This time, when news of Yellowstone's wonders reached Washington, the federal government acted quickly, creating the world's first national park — to protect what had long been dismissed as myth. Indeed, within Yellowstone are two-thirds of the geysers and half of the geothermal features known on Earth.

# BUTCH & SUNDANCE

THEIR REAL NAMES WERE FORGETTABLE, but Butch Cassidy and the Sundance Kid got their nicknames from time spent in Wyoming — Butch from a short stint as a butcher in Rock Springs, and Sundance from his first arrest in the town of Sundance. Famous for robbing banks and trains, Butch went to prison only once — 18 months for stealing horses.

Although they were known for a lack of violence *during* robberies, gang members did kill several people, often during the pursuits that ensued.

In 1901, Butch and Sundance journeyed to South America, where they spent several years working both within and outside the law. According to legend, they died in a shootout in southern Bolivia. Many reports, however, including those from family members, insist that both men returned to the United States, where each lived in anonymity for nearly 30 years.

THE HISTORY CHANNEL.

the states

## THE STATES » PART I

### CALIFORNIA

A love affair with cars ... 1848 discovery of gold at Sutter's Mill ... the San Francisco Earthquake of 1906

### NORTH CAROLINA

The mysterious disappearance of 117 colonists ... tobacco: North Carolina's cash crop ... historic sit-in at Woolworth's whites-only lunch counter

### KANSAS

Violent pro- and anti-slavery clashes that led to the nickname "Bleeding Kansas" ... the cattle boomtown of Dodge City ... Wichita as home to aircraft pioneers

### NEW HAMPSHIRE

Losing the Old Man of the Mountain ... the first colony to take military action against England ... small state with big political influence

### WEST VIRGINIA

Bridge-jumping at its best ... Virginia counties that chose to form their own state ... one of the largest uprisings in America since the Civil War

## THE STATES » PART II

### TEXAS

This state's Latino flavor ... the Alamo — a well-remembered U.S. defeat that overshadowed a later victory ... the record-breaking discovery of oil in 1901

### MASSACHUSETTS

The arrival of the Puritans ... Harvard's unique Statue of Three Lies ... Massachusetts' maritime traditions

### ARKANSAS

Teenage martyr for the Confederates ... Hot Springs and the mob ... the costly entrance into Little Rock's Central High School that broke the back of segregation

### IOWA

Where farmers rub elbows with would-be presidents ... corn — the crop that fuels the state, and the world ... an unknown painter who launched an art movement

### DELAWARE

First in line in the parade ... another famous midnight ride for independence ... the nation's No. 1 manufacturer of gunpowder

## THE STATES » PART III

### NEW YORK

New Amsterdam — the Dutch trading settlement that became New York ... the engineering marvel of the Erie Canal ... the state that perfected the skyscraper

### OREGON

Oregon Trail — the famous route westward ... aerial assault by the Japanese ... one of the nation's leaders in timber production

### LOUISIANA

French Canadians and Cajun ... the battles that saved (and lost) control of the Mississippi River ... Katrina and its historic antecedent: the Great Flood of 1927

### NEW MEXICO

Legends of New Mexico: UFOs and Billy the Kid ... weapons research in the high desert ... a holiday for burning last year's bad memories

### VERMONT

The first state constitution to outlaw slavery ... the state that Confederates attacked — via Canada ... one local ice-cream company that hit the big time

## THE STATES » PART IV

### NEW JERSEY

Christmas night 1776 and the crossing of the Delaware River ... the early days of "lights, camera, action" ... boardwalk beginnings in Atlantic City

### ARIZONA

One of nature's masterpieces: the Grand Canyon ... Tombstone, Arizona, and its famous gunfight ... where astronauts train for lunar landings

### KENTUCKY

Home of a very famous baseball bat ... the exploits of Daniel Boone ... "the most exciting 2 minutes in sports"

### OKLAHOMA

Trail of Tears ... where settlers raced across the prairie to claim land ownership ... escape from the Dust Bowl — another of the nation's great migrations

### ALASKA

Dog sledding and the famous Iditarod ... the first (and only) foreign invasion of U.S. soil since 1812 ... 1.3 million barrels of oil a day

## DVD DISC TWO

### THE STATES » PART V

**PENNSYLVANIA**
The country's most famous groundhog ... an underground fire that's been burning for more than 40 years ... building a steel empire

**MINNESOTA**
U.S. land that you can't reach without going through Canada? ... the "black gold" of the Mesabi Range ... the country's most well-known imaginary town

**HAWAII**
The state's tumultuous entrance into the union ... the Purple Heart Battalion ... surfing: the sport that embodies Hawaiian culture

**SOUTH CAROLINA**
First southern State to secede ... first successful submarine attack ... Gullah — a unique blend of English and indigenous West African languages

**MONTANA**
Annual celebration of a hometown daredevil ... dinosaur bones and echoes of *Jurassic Park* ... the "Last Stand" for General Custer and several Native-American tribes

### THE STATES » PART VI

**FLORIDA**
The land no one wanted ... the $30 million railroad that is no longer ... launching pad for "one giant leap for mankind"

**INDIANA**
Tippecanoe and Tyler Too ... the original "motor city" and its fastest race ... the capture of public enemy No. 1

**WASHINGTON**
Launching point for the Klondike/Alaska Gold Rush ... airplane assembly on a huge scale ... the terrifying eruption of Mount St. Helens

**UTAH**
Mormon expansion: from this country to Mexican territory, and back again ... the lake so salty no fish can survive ... land-speed records on the Bonneville Salt Flats

**RHODE ISLAND**
Where license-plate numbers are kept in the family ... a home for those seeking religious tolerance ... the millionaires' playground

### THE STATES » PART VII

**ILLINOIS**
Where Lincoln was challenged to a duel ... the state with its own pyramids ... the hunt for "Scarface" — Al Capone

**CONNECTICUT**
History of the "Charter Oak" ... the one-manned "Turtle" submarine ... the shipbuilding roots of Connecticut's insurance industry

**NEVADA**
A famous writer who first sought his fortune in the silver lodes ... Las Vegas: more hotel rooms than any other city in the world ... the mystery behind "Area 51"

**MISSISSIPPI**
The rise of King Cotton ... the country's first two African-American senators ... birthplace of the blues

**WYOMING**
The state that refused to join the union without women's suffrage ... unbelievable "myths" about Yellowstone that proved to be true ... Butch Cassidy and the Sundance Kid

## DVD DISC THREE

### THE STATES » PART VIII

**VIRGINIA**
Birthplace of eight presidents ... the burning of Jamestown ... five concentric rings, five stories tall, one of the largest office buildings in the world: the Pentagon

**OHIO**
Mother of Modern Presidents ... the flaming Cuyahoga River and creation of the Environmental Protection Agency ... the "Gravity Grand Prix"

**IDAHO**
The world's largest baked potato ... the nation's highest falls and deepest gorge ... where pursuit of gold turned to silver

**ALABAMA**
An obscure town that produced great sound ... the county that tried to secede from Alabama ... where Rosa Parks refused to give up her seat

**NORTH DAKOTA**
Teddy Roosevelt's love for the environment ... the safest state in the nation? ... where immigrants homesteaded the harsh climate of the plains

### THE STATES » PART IX

**MICHIGAN**
Largest state-forest system in the country ... the underwater tunnel to Canada ... home of the American auto industry

**TENNESSEE**
Davy Crockett: king of the wild frontier ... Nashville's country-music empire ... a distinctive whiskey that's known the world over

**MAINE**
The coveted crustacean ... the nation's first Prohibition law ... where wilderness lovers buy their boots — and more

**MISSOURI**
Earthquakes and land acquisitions that altered Missouri's shape ... pivotal role in America's westward expansion ... the beer delivered to the president via Clydesdales

**SOUTH DAKOTA**
The world's largest outdoor "bird feeder"... gold discovered in Native-American sacred land ... Mount Rushmore and a tribute to Chief Crazy Horse

### THE STATES » PART X

**GEORGIA**
Where Confederacy heroes are carved in stone ... Sherman's scorched-earth march across the state ... Dr. Mays' lifelong influence on Dr. Martin Luther King Jr.

**COLORADO**
The country's first organized rodeo ... history of the Denver Mint ... the fortified bunker that's thousands of feet below ground

**WISCONSIN**
Bratwurst, mustard and cheese from "America's Dairyland"... beverages that built Milwaukee ... final resting place for sunken ships

**NEBRASKA**
The country's first homesteader, in 1862 ... "Buffalo Bill's Wild West" ... the nation's only unicameral legislature

**MARYLAND**
A northern state torn by Confederate sympathies ... the song that memorializes our nation's flag ... the unique piece of land with federal status but without states' rights

EACH PART, LENGTH: 44 minutes
PRODUCED BY: Actuality Productions